South Islander

(Memoirs of a cruising dog)

Trials, triumphs and tales of cruising the British Columbia coast

By Amanda Spottiswoode
With illustrations by Molly March

Includes maps of dog walks from the San Juan Islands to Desolation Sound

Produced by:

FriesenPress

Suite 300 – 852 Fort Street

Victoria, BC, Canada V8W 1H8

www.friesenpress.com

Distributed to the trade by The Ingram Book Company

Table of Contents

This book is dedicated in loving memory to
Rosalind Russell aka Roz

February 1997 – December 2012

Acknowledgments

Patsy Siemens for editing grammar and punctuation
Bert Tatham for downloading topographical maps of all the walks
Nick Hutchinson for reading the first draft
Tomas Navratil for allowing me to use stories of his misspent youth
Roz and Moby for being the inspiration for this book

As we paddled the dinghy out from the beach, I glanced around Long Harbour, eyeing the anchored boats with interest − a couple of gleaming white sailboats with trim sail-covers, and a dilapidated wooden boat draped in fraying tarps. I crossed my fingers, hoping we were heading for the sailboat with the dashing blue graphics on its hull. Not so. My heart sank as the dinghy swung towards the shabby wooden boat and we came alongside. A peeling wooden sign fixed to the stern displayed the name of the boat − *South Islander.* Tomas went aboard, unstrung the tarps and my dog and I climbed over the side. I was unsuccessfully looking for something complimentary to say when Tomas slid back the hatch and I looked below. It was love at first sight − and I'm not talking about Tomas!

During an unhappy childhood largely spent locked up in an English boarding school, I had escaped into the world of Arthur Ransome, an English writer who wrote a series of books published in the 1930s and 40s. The first book in the series is titled *Swallows and Amazons* and features a group of children who camp, sail and have adventures with the gentle guidance of perfect parents. In subsequent books their adventures take them around the world on a number of vessels, described in detail. And here was a composite version of those boats. Not a piece of plastic or fibreglass in sight, rather a hooped cabin roof resembling a gypsy caravan, cozy stove, shelves, bunks and cabinets all handcrafted in various woods. Slightly shabby, definitely in need of a good clean, but nonetheless a boat with sufficient character to speak to all those child-hood dreams.

In fact, sometimes I have to pinch myself that I ended up here at all, realizing those dreams and living a life that, as a child, I could not even have imagined. I was always a bit of a misfit, buried in the world of Arthur Ransome and fantasizing about camping and sailing adventures I never had the chance to experience, but at the age of thirteen I managed to persuade my father to enrol me in sailing lessons. This he did, by signing me up for a week-long course at a place called Raven's Ait, an island in the Thames near to Kew, the suburb of London where we lived. Raven's Ait was a centre for teaching sailing to naval cadets, and they occasionally offered courses to civilian kids. I remember being interviewed by the Commander, who asked me why I wanted to learn to sail. I hesitantly mentioned *Swallows and Amazons*, and he immediately understood the fascination those books had for me. So I went to naval school for a week, slept in a dormitory and moved from dorm, to meals, to classroom lessons, to actual sailing all at the blast of a whistle. I loved it – except for the bit where I had to capsize a dinghy in the frigid and murky waters of the Thames in order to get my certificate. I put that one off until the last minute, but did it eventually. The water was very cold, and as far as I can remember we weren't even wearing lifejackets. None of Arthur Ransome's characters are ever shown wearing lifejackets, so I didn't find that odd. Can you imagine nowadays sending a child out into the middle of a river and dumping them overboard with no PFD?

In the chapters to follow you will read about Tomas, the man who, coming from a land-locked country as a penniless refugee, dreamed of and built a boat that is a marvel of crafts-manship and the sturdiest and safest boat on the water. It could, and did, survive a hurricane. You will read about the incredible beauty and history of our coast and the characters, past and present, who have inhabited it. And you will read about the boating mishaps that can catch even the most experienced boaters unawares.

That day when I first set foot on *South Islander* was the start of more than a decade of cruising up and down the B.C. coast on our beloved boat, whose permanent moorage is at our home on Long Harbour, Salt Spring Island. There have been many improvements and upgrades over the years, but the spirit of the boat remains the same – not too smart, definitely low-tech, but sturdy and safe with all the fairly basic comforts one could wish for. I think Arthur Ransome would have thoroughly approved of *South Islander*.

This book is for those of you, with or without dogs, who know the coast as well as we do, but perhaps have yet to discover some of the walks we have explored. It's for those of you boaters who may never set a foot ashore but who will enjoy the stories of our cruising triumphs and mishaps and it's for those who have never cruised the waters of British Columbia but who may be inspired to do so after reading this book.

Since I have never cruised without dogs, they are a central theme to the book. Our two Jack Russell Terriers have added immeasurably to our experiences and given us endless entertain-ment, not to mention exercise along the way. We would never have "discovered" many of the places I write about if we had not had the dogs on board, and they are the inspiration for this book.

Chapter One

1998: The Year of Being Crazy in Love and Running Aground

It was our first cruise. A couple of days in the Southern Gulf Islands – a trial run to see if we could get on well enough to tackle a full-blown summer cruise up the Coast. So far everything had been going extremely well. We had anchored in Reef Harbour adjacent to Cabbage and Tumbo Islands, which in turn lie just off the eastern side of Saturna Island. It was early June and the weather had been perfect, sunny and warm, with romantic glowing sunsets thrown in for good measure. Roz, my Jack Russell Terrier, seemed to like the whole boating experience, especially the part when the anchor went down and she was invited to jump into the dinghy and head ashore for walkies.

Now it was time to head back to Salt Spring Island. Being the gentleman he is, Tomas had invited me to stay in bed with a cup and tea and my book while he got us under way. The early morning sun streamed in through the forehatch as the boat chugged on its way between Tumbo and Saturna Islands, heading around East Point and into Boundary Pass. Suddenly I noticed that the light had dimmed and a breath of chilly air wafted down the hatch. I pulled on a sweater and headed up the companionway. Gone was the breathtaking vista of ocean, islands and distant mountains. Instead, we were floating in what appeared to be a diminishing circle of water with fuzzy walls. Fog had descended on us with breathtaking speed. I wasn't terribly concerned, as I knew I had an experienced captain in charge and I was fairly confident that he would get us back home safely.

In those days we had neither a GPS nor radar. Just the old fashioned navigational tools, i.e. a compass, charts and a rather elderly knot meter, which whirled a few times and then stopped working altogether. Despite the fact that I'd been sailing for years and knew the basics of navigation, in this instance I was quite willing to be the passive passenger and watched as Tomas did some competent looking calculations with the tools on hand. We set off heading in what we thought was the general direction of Fulford Harbour on Salt Spring Island. The sun was trying to break through the fog, which resulted in an eerie glow penetrating into our little bubble of clear water. A couple of Dall porpoises popped up and swam along with us for a while, adding to our sense of having been transported to another world.

After blindly motoring along for a couple of hours, a wall of black suddenly and alarmingly loomed up a few feet in front of our bow. We did the nautical equivalent of slamming on the brakes; that is, we rammed the engine into reverse. As we slid to a halt, the black wall revealed itself as a rock cliff topped with trees. Someone had moved an island! Or could it be that we weren't where we thought we were? Some hurried consultation with the chart ensued, but we remained pretty much clueless as to where we were. Slowly we inched ahead looking for rocks and hoping we were heading through a channel and not into a bay.

Suddenly, as if a giant extractor had sucked it up into the atmosphere, the fog lifted and it immediately became clear that we were many miles south of where we thought we were. In fact we were in among the islands that lie off Sidney on Vancouver Island. A veritable maze of reefs, islets and narrow passages that we had negotiated by pure dumb luck. We spent the rest of the voyage back to Fulford Harbour figuring out what went wrong. It transpired that Tomas had been estimating our speed based on the rpm of the old engine which had recently been replaced with a newer and faster model. We had actually been travelling much faster than we thought, which had resulted in us going way past our intended change of course point. So let this serve as a cautionary tale to all of us who head out on the water in less than perfect conditions – even the most experienced can find themselves in trouble.

I think now would be an appropriate time to tell you a little bit about the boat and the man who built her. Tomas was born to educated, middle-class parents in Czechoslovakia just after the war. They had had their business, home and most of their worldly possessions confiscated by the communist regime. His father was put into a factory painting military vehicles, and his mother was sent to work in a railway yard switching trains. Tomas and his two brothers were brought up in a one-bedroom apartment in Prague, but his grandmother lived in the country and the times they spent with her were idyllic.

Some of their adventures are legendary. My favourite story is of the time Tomas and his older brother decided to take a pair of duelling pistols from a castle that was open to the public. Tomas, being the smallest, was delegated to remain hidden after closing time, when all the visitors left and the castle was locked. He then removed the pistols from the wall and retreated to the cellar, which had been previously cased out by the boys. They had discovered a small opening that led out through the massive walls to the moat. I've seen the drop, and it's daunting. I can only imagine what it must have looked like to an 8-year-old boy as he scrambled down and into the arms of his brother. They took the pistols back to their grandmother's house, but were quickly found out and confessed to their crime. Their parents and grandmother were understandably concerned about admitting the theft to the communist authorities, doubtless imagining the boys being shipped off to the salt mines. Eventually, the guns were packaged up and posted back to the castle anonymously from the central post office in Prague. When we visited the Czech Republic in 2001, we toured the castle, and there were the pistols, back on the wall! That was just one in a long series of childhood pranks that included such adventures as manufacturing gunpowder in their grandmother's attic and almost blowing up the entire house.

Both Tomas and his older brother had a fascination with the native culture of North America and read anything they could get their hands on, though not much of this sort of literature was allowed by the communist regime. When Tomas was 11 and his older brother, Milos, was 14, Milos stowed away on a plane, having for inexplicable reasons decided he wanted to go to Cuba. He was discovered when the plane landed in Ireland and, as requested, was put on a plane to Cuba. When the plane landed for refuelling in Gander, Newfoundland, the crew advised him that Cuba was not the best place for him to end up. He would merely be trading one repressive regime for another, albeit one with a better climate. He got off the plane and thus became the youngest ever unaccompanied refugee in Canadian history.

Tomas followed his brother to Canada in 1969, and soon after headed for the West Coast. For someone who had been brought up in a land-locked country, he had a strange fascination for the ocean and had read countless seafaring tales. Without any training or experience, he decided to build a boat. And build it he did, in a junkyard in Squamish inhabited by a character named Junky Jim, who lived there with his 34 dogs.

South Islander is loosely designed along the lines of Hartley (a New Zealand boat design), but Tomas adapted the plans and made her a couple of feet longer by spreading the pre-sawn frames further apart. Thirty four feet long overall, nine feet wide at the widest point, she is constructed of two layers of 5/8 inch yellow and red cedar planking. It took a couple of years to finish the hull, as every time Tomas ran out of materials he had to go off to work in logging camps to earn the money for the next batch of lumber. We often joke that if he had taken that money and invested in real estate in Whistler, he would have made a fortune and been able to buy the boat of his dreams - thus saving himself the considerable effort involved in building South Islander.

It took three years to complete the hull and keels. One of the boat's most useful features is her twin bilge keels which means, as she only draws three feet, she can go into many places that are inaccessible to other boats. In addition, when she needs her bottom scrubbed, instead of paying haul out fees, we just put her up on the beach at high tide and wait for the tide to fall leaving her high and dry. Those twin keels are filled with an assortment of cement and scrap metal which gives her tremendous stability. In fact, Tomas got a bit overenthusiastic and once he saw how low in the water she floated, had to painstakingly chip out a portion of the ballast.

Once the hull was completed Tomas employed a crane to turn her right side up and put her in the water. Now she was a shell that floated and he began a further two years of finishing the interior, the solid teak deck and the mast and rigging. He named her *South Islander* after her New Zealand design and eventually left Squamish and began thirty years of cruising the coast.

At the time he built the boat in the early 1970s, Tomas was embracing the hippie life-style. Photos show him with bare feet and curly hair that grew straight out in a blond "Afro". Eventually the boat was finished, but as anyone who has ever owned a boat knows, the job is never actually finished and it's always a work in progress. There is no job on the boat that Tomas can't handle, from installing a holding tank, to rewiring the boat, to endlessly scraping, sanding and varnishing the woodwork. It is truly a labour of love.

When I came along, Tomas was just out of his first marriage. For the purposes of this book, we will call his first wife the Diva. In fact, she was an opera singer so she actually was a diva, but in reality she was a Diva with a most affirmative capital. Shortly before they were divorced there was a fire on the boat. The Diva had left the stove turned up to the maximum while the boat was tied to their neighbour's dock in Long Harbour. At that point the thermostat on the stove malfunctioned and started a fire. The neighbour noticed smoke billowing out of the chimney and had the presence of mind to stick a hose down the chimney, rather than opening the hatch. This action undoubtedly saved the boat from total annihilation. The interior of the boat, which had been coated in thick black soot, was cleaned shortly after the fire, but the cabin roof and some of the bulkhead is still blackened. After years of sanding and cleaning the slight charring remains and, in our opinion, adds to the character of the boat.

So here we were in the summer of 1998, heading off on our first big cruise to Desolation Sound. This was a big ambition of mine, as for many years while living in Vancouver, I'd crewed on large racing boats. Every summer the owners of these boats abandoned their faithful crews and headed off cruising with their families. During the racing season we had endured adverse conditions including, but not limited to, chipping ice off the decks prior to racing, sitting for hours in pouring rain and flat calm in the middle of English Bay and hurling ourselves from side to side of the open deck while being liberally doused with cold sea water. Then, during the summer cruising season, the skippers' families, not us, got to enjoy balmy, weather and spectacular scenery while lazing on the deck. Finally, my turn had come!

I took on the provisioning of the boat for our cruise. Here was an opportunity to indulge in all my childhood food favourites, with a nod to my old friend Arthur Ransome, who described in great detail the meals cooked by one of his characters, Mate Susan. We have no oven, and cook on a two-burner propane camp stove and a barbeque, which in the early days was a portable model we set up on a cookie tray on the deck. For the first few years we didn't have a functioning fridge either, as it, along with the original stove and oven, were victims of the Diva's fire. We used the old fridge as an icebox, and along with a few day's supply of frozen meat, this kept our provisions cool for a several days. I love cooking on the boat. There is no pressure to create gourmet meals, but somehow every meal seems gourmet anyway. Of course, even the simplest meal tastes sublime when consumed on deck on a beautiful summer evening with a stunning backdrop of mountains and ocean.

On that first cruise I discovered the basic difference between racing and cruising. In racing, it doesn't matter how much or little wind there is, it's all about getting round those marks, no matter how long it takes and how unpleasant it is along the way. Cruising is all about being out on the water in the most enjoyable way possible. This means that if there is too much wind, we try and stay tucked up in some cozy cove; if there is not enough and we want to get to the next spot, we motor. Actually, I have to admit that there is nothing I like better than motoring in a flat calm at a sedate 6 knots, lounging with a good book in my hammock strung between the mast and the forestay.

Any worries I may have had about getting along with Tomas in the close quarters of the boat were soon allayed. As a child, I was constantly trying to get my sister and my best friend to join me on my camping adventures. They were the most reluctant participants. I have a photograph of me sitting with a clipboard outside a tent, making lists of supplies a la Mate Susan, while Caroline and Geraldine loll sullenly in the background. They were simply not interested. But at last, 30 years later, I had met my match. That first summer I started reading aloud from *Swallows and Amazons* and Tomas instantly embraced the tales of sailing, camping and exploring. The coast of British Columbia would have been an ideal setting for an Arthur Ransome adventure, and we often imagined one of his boats nosing into some secret cove on a remote and uninhabited island. Having a dog aboard adds an extra element to the cruising experience, as one has to go ashore no matter what the weather, and once ashore you might as well explore.

A word or two here about the aforementioned dog. In 1998, when I met Tomas, I owned a young, rough-haired Jack Russell Terrier named Rosalind Russell, aka Roz. To be perfectly honest, Roz is not desperately keen on the sailing part of the boating experience. She has a tendency to shiver in the cockpit when we are underway, even though she is warmly attired in her personal flotation device and covered with blankets in cool weather. However, once she hears the engine change tone and the boat slows down, she is up on deck and eyeing the dinghy. No sooner have we dropped anchor she executes a huge pier-head jump into the dinghy and waits expectantly, gazing towards shore and quivering in anticipation.

And here's a hint for those of you who have never cruised with dogs but are thinking about it, or are new to the experience and perhaps have not discovered what I am about to reveal. Dogs can go a long, long time between bathroom breaks. That first summer cruising we were not party to this vital tidbit of doggie lore. We would walk Roz last thing at night, often in the pitch black, negotiating getting on and off the dinghy and finding a suitable place to land by the light of a flashlight. Then around 5 a.m., when Roz woke up and started looking expectantly at us, we would dress and row ashore in the chilly dawn to repeat the process. But then we started to notice something interesting. While most of us would be hard pressed to go an entire night without a trip to the bathroom, and would surely be desperate for relief after 7 or 8 hours, Roz would jump ashore and start exploring – exploring <u>before</u> taking advantage of the shore facilities. This initial sniff around could go on for 10 or 15 minutes before she actually got down to business. Clearly she wasn't desperate. Since then we have heard from other dog owners that dogs can often go 10 to 12 hours, sometimes even longer, without any signs of distress. Nowadays we ignore any early morning whining and enjoy our tea before heading ashore at a reasonable time.

Our voyage in 1998 has come to be known as The Summer of being Crazy in Love and Running Aground. We did it twice. The first time was on Rebecca Spit on Quadra Island. We had had a long and miserably rough journey up Georgia Strait, stopping briefly in Campbell River for diesel. The stretch of coast on the western side of Georgia Strait, between Nanaimo and Campbell River, has a paucity of places to duck into, and we only had 12 days on this trip. Desolation Sound was our destination so we gritted our teeth and battled on. The weather was getting worse and the light was fading as we rounded Cape Mudge on Quadra Island and headed north towards Heriot Bay. Suddenly the wall of trees on our port side disappeared and the lights of Heriot Bay showed clearly. We must have reached the end of the spit and turned sharply to port, heading for the lights. A couple of minutes later there was a dreadful crunch and we ground to a halt. Obviously not the end of the spit after all. Once again, our twin keels came in handy. The very bottom of the keels are steel railway lines, and they were grinding and banging alarmingly as the boat lifted and dropped in the choppy waters. I was moments away from calling the Coast Guard, but Tomas put the engine in reverse and the boat ground its way backwards off the rocks with the most dreadful noise. I was sure there must be a hole in the bottom of the boat, and in many other, less sturdy vessels, that would likely have been the result of this mishap. We made way again and within a few minutes discovered the vital clue as to when to turn left. The very obvious light at the end of the spit that is, of course, clearly marked on the chart.

The second mishap was in Prideaux Haven. I had heard much about this fabled cove. It had been billed as a paradise anchorage in Desolation Sound, and I really, really wanted to go there. We headed in, this time carefully checking the chart. It appeared that there was a ledge, which at that particular stage of the tide we should be able to cross into Laura Cove. We crept in as I stood watch on the bow. The waters were crystal clear and I could plainly see the bottom, when all of a sudden that bottom shelved steeply, and we bumped gently aground. Tomas' face registered a series of emotions – embarrassment being the primary one. Here he was trying to impress his new girlfriend with his superior boating skills and he had run us aground, not once but twice. We were able to back off, hoping not too many people were watching, and checked the chart again. This time our fault lay in using a very old chart, which showed a depth that there clearly was not. Perhaps the channel had silted up over the years, and a newer chart showed the correct depth. But in any case this was a lesson learned: always use a current version of your charts and get rid of all those dated 1929! In fact, that has been our only visit to Prideaux Haven as we found it overcrowded with a plethora of huge boats hogging the best spots. There was a flotilla of six enormous power boats rafted up together and stern tied to a small islet. When we eventually found a spot to anchor and were rowing towards the islet to walk the dog, they yelled at us to stay away as they had seen a bear there earlier. These floating palaces sported a forest of bristling fishing gear, and our suspicion was that they had caught way over their allowable limit of salmon and did not want anyone coming close enough to see their illegal fish processing "factory". Discretion being the better part of valour, and given my slightly unreasonable fear of large predatory animals, we took the dog ashore elsewhere.

One place we have never been back to is Evans Bay on Read Island. It is a quiet and picturesque anchorage, but we had an unpleasant experience there. Tomas had regaled me with stories of crabs fighting to get into the trap so that they could provide us with a gourmet dinner, doused in butter and lemon, and I naively thought it really was going to be that easy. After checking the chart for the right sort of bottom (fairly sandy and shallow being the best, deep and rocky – no hope), we decided to try our luck in Evans Bay. We lowered our brand new crab trap and attached the float before heading ashore. It really is a beautiful place, with old logging roads that over decades have morphed into grassy lanes – perfect for dog walking. Right up at the head of the bay we went ashore and found, not only an overabundance of blackberry bushes loaded with ripe berries, but also an abandoned orchard with ripe apples just begging to be turned into blackberry and apple compote. Loaded with fruit we headed back to the boat, looking forward to hauling up our trap bursting with crustaceans, only to discover that our float was no longer attached to the trap, and the trap was presumably resting on the bottom of the bay. We were extremely puzzled. Tomas is a master at nautical knotting and there was absolutely no chance that his knot had come undone. We scoured the cove and finally spotted our float at the very head of the bay. Closer inspection revealed the line had been cut – there was no question that it was a deliberate act. We can only assume that someone felt that the bay and its resident crabs were their property, not to be harvested by visiting boaters.

That summer our cruise was limited by time, but that was enough to give me a taste for cruising, and long enough to make it to some of the most beautiful spots in the Desolation Sound area. Some of those places we visited the first year have been on our itinerary every year since. We never ever get tired of Savary Island with its sandy trails and spectacular beaches. The anchorages that have nearby lakes are also favourites; swimming in the fresh water is wonderful after a few showerless days on the boat. That first year we swam in Cassel Lake in Teakerne Arm and Unwin Lake in Tenedos Bay, and discovered that each of those spots has delightful walks from the shore up to the lakes – perfect for dogs anxious for shore leave after a long stretch at sea.

At the end of that first cruise, Roz had gained her sea legs and expressed great interest in further expeditions, and Tomas and I were only too happy to oblige.

Chapter Two

1999: THE YEAR OF BEING CRAZY IN
LOVE AND RUNNING OUT OF FUEL

1999 started with a bang – literally. The bang of 7 ½ tons of boat thudding onto the rocks on the east side of Long Harbour. It was early February, and the normally tranquil waters of the harbour had been whipped into a frenzy by a huge south easterly winter gale. We were not yet living on our waterfront property as the house was unfinished, but the boat had been residing happily on her mooring buoy for several years. Our neighbour, George, saw her part company with the buoy and called Tomas, who came rushing from his office in town. By the time he got there her mast was jammed up against a neighbouring dock, but he managed to climb aboard and start the engine. As it was winter she was swathed in an enveloping boat cover and, despite taking time to jam a trailing line under the canvas, the inevitable happened. As he unsuccessfully tried to steer her to the middle of the harbour, the line blew free and any boater will guess what happened next. Horrible thudding ensued and as the line wrapped itself around the propeller shaft, the engine quit and Tomas found himself adrift with no steerage, no engine and, by now, five-foot waves. Later we heard that the winds actually reached hurricane force that day. He was quickly blown across the harbour and onto the opposite shore where, somewhat optimistically, he jumped overboard into waist-deep water and attempted to hold her off the beach. Fortunately George had called the Coast Guard and they came along just in time to prevent Tomas being crushed to death, got the boat off and tied her to a nearby dock.

This story is a testimony to the strength and sturdiness of *South Islander*. Tomas had built her for ocean cruising and we are in no doubt that a fibreglass boat, or indeed many wooden boats, would have cracked like an eggshell on that rocky beach. Piecing events together we discovered that the rudder had actually broken off before Tomas even got on board, so he stood no chance of steering her anywhere. We found the broken-off rudder many days later at the head of the harbour. In addition to the missing rudder she sustained significant damage to the propeller shaft and many of the adjacent fittings. The interior was a shambles, and even the mirror firmly screwed to the wall had been shaken out of its fittings and lay in shards.

Many a boater would have been daunted by the prospect of repairing the damage. Unfortunately at this time we had no insurance, a matter swiftly rectified once the repairs were complete. Tomas just took this mishap in stride and built a new rudder, starting with four sheets of plywood nailed to the floor of our unfinished house. Many weeks of shaping, fibre glassing, sanding and painting followed, before the boat was put up on the beach on her twin bilge keels and the rudder was refitted to the hull. In fact, the new rudder turned out to be much better than the old one – I guess Tomas had read a few more books since making the original 15 years earlier!

At this point I think I will philosophize a little about lists. I am an inveterate list-maker; lists of things to do, things to buy, places to go, people to call – the list goes on. At the very beginning of our cruising life together, I began to make lists in the logbook. How naïve I was. I probably thought that by putting things on the list, they would somehow, magically, get done immediately, if not sooner. Usually at the end of each cruising season I made a list of things that I would like done before the beginning of the next season. A perfect example is the cockpit table. We used to put a tablecloth down on the deck and eat off that. But I had an image of a table that we and friends could sit round, sipping a glass of wine and gazing at the sunset. I thought it would be a simple thing to make. It took six years to get checked off that list. First Tomas had to think about it for a year or so, and then he had to design it, choose the right sort of wood and the right sort of fittings and then finally craft it. When I eventually got it I was thrilled; like everything Tomas does it is a work of art. But it was a very long time coming. Oh, and it takes someone with an engineering degree to put it up and stow it away, but it is so, so beautiful and I suppose things like that can't be done in a rush.

Other lists have included such things as "make propane legal", a process that involved building a beautiful teak chest for the propane tank; "install holding tank" (more about that one later) and "redo electrics". I had no idea what that entailed until I saw Tomas crawling in the bowels of the boat leading a spaghetti-like mass of wires up, down, through and around. Magically, we can now listen to music in bed and turn the system off by flipping a switch on the bedside bulkhead. Roz just never listened when we asked her to press the off button on the stereo in the saloon! The best thing about lists is when you finally get to check something off – even if it takes several years.

I also keep lists and tables of all the places we go, including mileage, stops of interest and weather. When I started cruising with Tomas, there was just over 100 hours on the new engine; there are now over 1500, faithfully recorded every time we fill up with diesel. There's just something about the boat that makes me want to record every detail of our time on her.

Our 1999 cruise took up back to Desolation Sound and beyond. At least that's what we planned. I had heard much about the dreaded Seymour Narrows, the gateway to Johnstone Strait, where would we supposedly encounter pods of whales frolicking around the boat. Having heard about boats that had foundered in the rapids, and dire warnings about only traversing them at the nanosecond the current went slack, I was distinctly apprehensive about going through in anything smaller than a cruise ship. However, Tomas assured me that it was quite safe. So with the carrot of those whales dangling in front of me, I agreed to go.

We stopped at Campbell River and filled up with diesel before approaching Seymour Narrows at exactly slack water. What an anticlimax! It was like a millpond and could quite safely have been traversed in a canoe. Piece of cake, I thought, as we headed north up Johnstone Strait.

We stopped in Kelsey Bay overnight and then continued our northward voyage the next day. My complacency about how the perils of Seymour Narrows and Johnstone Strait were over exaggerated faded as the weather began to deteriorate and we started bucking an increasing wind funnelling down the Strait. We were about 5 miles past Port Neville when the engine quit. The middle of Johnstone Strait in an increasing gale is not the best place to be when you are drifting engineless with the wind on your nose. Tomas did some tinkering and the engine coughed to life. We decided to head into Port Neville and, with the wind now behind us, raised the sail to help us along. Just as we thought the crisis was over, the engine quit again and the wind dropped just as we encountered a strong current pushing us away from Port Neville and back into the middle of the Strait. I'm not quite sure how we did it, but we managed to limp into the Government Dock as the engine gave a last wheezy cough and died completely.

Port Neville is a very interesting place, and at that time there were three generations of women living in what by any standards is a remote and inaccessible place. We met Lilly, the matriarch, in whose kitchen I sat as she told me tales of her life on the coast. We also met Lorna her daughter, who along with her granddaughter, ran the Post Office. I found the presence of a Post Office quite extraordinary, but it remains as a reminder of the days when this part of the coast was a bustling place, with fishermen, hand-loggers and homesteaders coming and going. In addition to the separate homes of Lilly and Lorna, the tiny settlement boasted an enormous log building that had at one time been a general store serving the surrounding area. Built in 1924 and operating until 1960 it how houses an art gallery and museum.

That day in Port Neville I had confirmation that the British Columbia coast can be a dangerous place. As an immigrant from England, and despite having lived in British Columbia for the past 30 years, I have a phobia about large wild animals. Even though I lived for many years in rural areas where *Ursus americanus* are common, over those 30 years I have probably seen fewer than half a dozen bears, and no cougars at all. Regardless, I have an unreasonable fear that a large man-eating animal is lurking behind every tree. And, of course, a 20-pound Jack Russell Terrier would make a very tasty treat. Tomas thinks I'm being paranoid but Lorna told us the story of the day she was walking with her then six-year-old daughter across her front yard (and I mean her front yard, between the garden gate and the house) when a cougar appeared out of nowhere and grabbed the child. She managed to fight off the animal before it was able to harm the little girl, but warned us that bears and cougars were very common in the area and to be careful walking the dog. I needed no second bidding and Roz got the most perfunctory of walks as I peered nervously into the dense bush surrounding the settlement.

Tomas started to investigate the engine failure, doing all sorts of mysterious things in the bowels of the boat, and after eliminating all other possible causes came to the humiliating conclusion that we had simply run out of fuel! Remember I mentioned filling up with fuel in Campbell River? When we looked at the amount of fuel we had taken on, we realized that we hadn't anywhere near filled up. The explanation was that there had been an air-lock which had given the false impression that the tank was full. We called this incident The Summer Of Being Crazy In Love And Running Out Of Fuel. The very nice people at Port Neville sold us enough fuel to get us to the next marina and we headed for Blind Channel Resort, leaving Johnstone Strait and those whales for another time.

In fact, it was another five years before we finally made it as far as Port McNeill. Anyone who cruises the coast and listens to the weather forecasts will be familiar with the summer weather on that part of the coast. While you may be sitting in a flat calm and brilliant sunshine in Georgia Strait, Johnstone Strait will consistently have gale force winds howling down from the north. Not what you want to head into for hours on end in a boat whose maximum speed is 6 miles an hour. Now, I know what you sailors are thinking – if there's wind and you have a sailboat, why not sail? Well, my idea of fun is definitely not beating up Johnstone Strait into 30 knots of wind, making about one mile an hour up the Strait – and it's about 40 miles from Chatham Point to Port MacNeill.

This may be a good time to talk a little bit about the tidal rapids that dot the coast. Having braved Seymour Rapids, I was prepared to listen when Tomas told me that it in fact made more sense to make use of the tidal currents. The idea is to traverse the rapids slightly after slack water when there's a bit of current going your way. He reminisced about the time he and the Diva had gone through Sechelt Rapids into Sechelt Inlet. Apparently they went through pretty close to maximum flood, going with a current of about 12 knots. They must have been hurtling through at about 18 knots in a boat whose maximum speed under power at that time was 5 ½ knots. The Diva thought it was a very exciting ride until they were on the other side, at which point she went pale and made Tomas swear they would never do anything so foolhardy again.

Anyway, he told me that he was much older and wiser now and would only ever use just a little bit of current to help us along. So I agreed, and after a night in Blind Channel we headed for Dent Rapids and Gillard Passage. If you look at a chart of that area you will clearly see something ominously marked "Devil's Hole". Well, I saw Devil's Hole that day, and I never want to see it again. As we swirled around its edge, I clutched Roz to my bosom and swore to read those tide tables myself next time. It would be slack or no go, as far as my dog and I were concerned!

We traversed most of the rapids on that part of the coast that year – Yuculta, Hole in the Wall, Beazley Passage and Dodd Narrows – all done at absolute slack. I had a vested interest in learning how to read the tide and current tables and calculate slack water to within 5 minutes. I retain a very healthy respect for the power of the unbelievable mass of water surging into and out of Georgia Strait through what amounts to the smallest of gaps.

The rating of our overnight anchorages was, and continues to be, measured in the quality of the dog walks. Sometimes the beauty of the anchorage is sufficient to make up for the paucity of walking opportunities, but there are so many places that have it all. The future stretched ahead; we had the rest of our lives to explore this beautiful coast, revisit old favourites and discover new ones. The only thing missing was a cruising companion for Roz, a matter that was to be remedied at the start of the new Millenium.

Chapter Three

2000: THE ADVENT OF MOBY

Moby Dick entered this world on May 12th, 2000. The day he was born, a 43-foot grey whale washed up on the beach in front of Moby's Marine Pub on Salt Spring Island. In addition to this, when Roz delivered her first-born, he had the perfectly shaped imprint of a whale's tail on his back. I knew this was the pup I was going to keep, and I named him in the first 30 seconds of his life.

Although Moby had slipped out with ease, as did the following two pups, Roz then stopped labouring and eventually she had to have a caesarean to deliver the remaining two puppies. It was all very traumatic. I was there when the vet did the operation, and although my first husband is a vet and I had assisted at many such surgeries, this was different. I was the epitome of an anxious and annoying pet owner. I decided that breeding was not for me. I was very happy with Moby, but that was the last time I was ever going to be personally involved in a doggie pregnancy.

For those of you that are familiar with the characteristics of Jack Russell Terriers, you will know that many of the breed have a reputation for being hyperactive, yappy and generally high maintenance dogs. You obviously have never met Moby, or his father Jake, two of the most laid back canines on the planet. We chose Jake for this very reason, as Roz had a certain tendency to those aforementioned JRT traits. Jake's owners at that time had an art gallery in downtown Ganges, and Jake could often be seen just hanging out on the sidewalk outside the gallery, observing the tourists and greeting prospective customers. Moby is a dog after his father's heart.

In 2000 we were living on the south end of Salt Spring while we were finishing our house on Long Harbour. As we were spending a lot of time at the new house, we didn't want to leave

Roz and her five puppies unattended. So every day we carted her, the litter of pups, food, newspapers, bed and crate from home to the worksite and set up the JRT nursery. As they grew, the job got more challenging. Now I was wrangling five puppies as they explored an ever-widening area.

We even took Roz and the pups on a boating expedition when they were only three weeks old. They lay in a box in the bottom of the cockpit and we motored to James Bay on Prevost Island for dinner. I like to think that Moby's love of the boat comes from such a positive first experience.

I was mightily relieved when the other four went to their new homes and we were left with Moby. From the very beginning he was the dream dog. He never chewed anything, was house-trained before we knew it, and had a demeanour that leads us to suppose that he is a thinker and philosopher rather than a chaser of deer and squirrels, as Roz most definitely is. Not that he hasn't been know to have the occasional lapse – more on that one in a later chapter.

Let's make no mistake about this; Moby is a very, very laid back dog. If he was a human he would be a cool dude, with shoulder length hair, a headband, would wear thrift store clothes, back-to-the-70s gear and drive a VW van. He would be into something that didn't require taxing himself too much, and spend a fair amount of time hanging out at the beach watching the girls.

Admittedly, Moby is a bit of a couch potato, while fortunately still retaining his youthful figure. He loves to sit propped up on a cushion watching TV, until his eyes droop and he slowly topples over into a supine position. His favourite TV show is Frasier as his role model is Eddie, and his favourite movie is My Dog Skip (for the same reason; same doggie actor).

Moby is a Prince among Pooches and we were smitten. It was hard to imagine how we had managed life as a one-dog family. We often joke that Moby's antics are better than cable TV. He makes us laugh several times a day and it's not because of any particular trick he does (except for a couple of "party tricks" he considers those kind of antics below his dignity), it's just he's so darn funny being himself.

One of his most endearing qualities is his modesty surrounding the business of pooing. Roz will just squat and poo wherever the spirit moves her, usually right in the middle of a path or in front of a picnicking family. Not so Moby. He will discreetly back up into a bush or tall grass and give us a look, which means he would rather we didn't watch. Sometimes he exhibits some rather odd behaviour. If there is a log, rock or tree that catches his fancy, he will reverse until his rear end is up against the obstacle and then slowly raise his hind legs up, and up, and up, until he is in effect doing a handstand. Then, and only then, he will deposit his load. Someone has suggested that this is to make other dogs that come along later think that a really big dog has been there.

We set off for our summer cruise at the beginning of August when Moby was less than 3 months old. His only concession to puppyhood was an inability to "hold it" through the night, so Tomas would get up and let him piddle on the deck once during the night. He never abused this privilege, and once he was able to hold it until the morning walk, never ever used the deck as a doggie loo.

He quickly adapted to shipboard life. Unlike Roz, who tends to quiver in the cockpit while we are underway, he liked to sleep on the port settee until we arrived at our destination, at which point, refreshed from his nap, he would enjoy a romp ashore before retiring to the same spot for his next nap.

We headed up the coast, via Nanaimo, Lasqueti and Texada and arrived at the gateway to Desolation Sound, and one of our favourite stops, Lund. I love Lund! It has it all; a friendly and well-run Government Dock, bakery, pub, store and laundry.

At about 2 am, Tomas headed up on deck for Moby's piddle break. I was roused from a deep sleep by his call to join him. I sleepily stuck my head out of the companionway and gasped in wonder. There was the most amazing display of Northern Lights that I have ever seen, even though I had at one time in lived Fort St. John, in the northern part of British Columbia. Sheets of shimmering light moved in waves across the sky, like a celestial curtain wafting in the breeze. We stared in awe for half an hour before heading back down below. That amazing experience would not have happened if it hadn't been for Moby.

We visited some of our favourite spots that year, including Heriot Bay and Manson's Landing, and some that were new to me. That year was the first time I went into Von Donop Inlet, which has to be one of the most beautiful spots on the coast. One can only imagine the early explorers heading into these uncharted waters and discovering such jewels as Von Donop. Of course, they didn't have doggie walks in mind and probably thought of it as just a dead end that meant that Cortez was one island, joined by the neck of land between Squirrel Cove and Von Donop. There is a beautiful trail that joins the two bodies of water, just the right length for a short walk after an "ocean crossing" and before settling down with a pre-dinner drink. I don't know if every boating dog behaves the same as ours, but it would be totally unthinkable to arrive in an anchorage after even a relatively short time "at sea" and not immediately, if not sooner, paddle the dogs ashore. Our dogs' attitude to the dinghy is that it is their personal water taxi, and they are quite clear that their taxi ride to shore is non-negotiable.

A less remote, but still favourite spot of ours, is Pender Harbour. After a long slog down Malaspina Strait, it is a great destination. We usually anchor in Garden Bay, handy for the pub and a short dinghy ride over to Madeira Park with all its amenities. Pender Harbour is then only a hop and a skip away from other Sunshine Coast favourites, such as Buccaneer Bay, a small marine park located on the sand spit on the southern tip of North Thormanby Island. This park has beautiful broad sandy beaches and warm waters. The large sheltered bay provides safe anchorage in most summer conditions.

We continued our journey south towards home and fetched up in Deep Bay on Jedediah Island. This place really rates very highly on my list of most favourite spots. The whole island is a Marine Park, with an abandoned farm and orchards, and several beautiful walks through forest and across open meadows. As the weather had deteriorated, and there was a south-easterly gale blowing, we decided to batten down the hatches for a couple of days. We had plenty of food, lots of books and the dogs were content with frequent trips ashore. On the third day, despite the fact that there was not much improvement in the weather, we decided to give it a try and headed out down Bull Passage and into the open waters of Georgia Strait.

This was a mistake. The waves were at least 8 feet high and the boat was pounding into them with alarming thuds. I peered below to check on Moby. Up until this time, while Roz never wanted to be below when we were underway, Moby, at the age of three months, was quite content to stretch on the port settee and be lulled to sleep by the gentle slapping of the water on the hull. However, this was different. Everything that had been stowed on the shelves was flying around the cabin, and alarmingly, there was no sign of Moby. I dodged flying plates and lurched through the cabin looking for him. I found him quivering, wedged in among the pipes in the head. There is an opening in the bulkhead at the end of the settee that goes through into the head and he had obviously slid through. I managed to extricate him from among the pipes and put him in the forepeak tucked in with pillows. Fighting increasing nausea I scrambled up the companionway. We were just off Squitty Bay at the very tip of Lasqueti and we considered scuttling in there for shelter, but we had never been there and the entrance is narrow. From where we were it presented as a wall of crashing waves and although we knew there was a way in, we weren't about to try it that day. Discretion being the better part of valour, we headed back to Deep Bay.

The bay was crammed with boaters. Someone had already taken our spot, and it looked like finding a place to anchor would be impossible. Then a man in a dinghy hove into view. With his help we found a narrow slot, anchored and stern tied and then our helper beetled off to assist the next boat coming in. We nicknamed him Keen Ken. He and his wife had been holed up in the bay for about a week, and were running out of groceries. His wife, obviously used to Ken's ways, was philosophical about the situation and informed us that they were managing fine on applesauce and cornflakes.

Upon arrival, I went below to check on our poor puppy, and discovered that he had been most decidedly sick all over the bed. And from that day to this, Moby is of like mind to Roz. When underway, the correct place for them to be is at the bottom of the cockpit, properly attired in their personal floatation devices.

Eventually the wind dropped and we were able to make our way home down Georgia Strait and back into our cozy anchorage in Long Harbour. Our third season on the boat was over and we would spend the wet, dark winter ahead dreaming about heading up the coast again – cruising is for the dogs!

Chapter Four

2001: ANCHORING SOUTH ISLANDER STYLE

There is a condition common among boaters called Twofootitus. This is the entirely harmless and amusing pastime of fantasizing about owning a bigger boat. In our case, after dreaming about a particular boat we have seen, we always come to the conclusion that we could never part with dear old *South Islander*. This time, however, had I had the proverbial winning lottery ticket in my wallet; our boat might well have been looking for a new slave to serve her. The boat was named *Papillon*, and she was tied up next to us at the government dock in Egmont, on the Sunshine Coast. She was a 43-foot double-ended ketch with the most beautifully appointed interior I've ever seen in a sailboat. And she sported a bathtub. Let me repeat that in case you didn't get it the first time – she had a bathtub! *South Islander's* bathing facilities are primitive to say the least. I thought we had attained the height of luxury when we acquired a Solar Shower, also known as a black plastic bag that hangs on the boom and requires a second person (other than the one taking the shower) to operate it. Imagine, if you will, shivering naked in the cockpit on a cool and breezy day. The shower operator, aka Tomas, damps you down with barely lukewarm water, you lather up in the fastest way possible and then rinse with a dribble of water before diving below to don every article of clothing on board. But here was a boat that had, not merely a shower, but a bath. I was in love! She also had a secret gun locker to hide a gun for fending off China Sea pirates; Arthur Ransome would have loved that. And . . . she was for sale! For a mere $195,000 US, she could be ours. I dreamed about that boat for years, actually until quite recently when I made the discovery that I wasn't that keen on sailing any more.

Don't get me wrong, I love, and will always love, boating. It's the sailing bit that has lost its appeal. I mean all those bits of rope littering the deck, all that trouble to raise and then lower the sails, and then when the sails do go up the boat takes on a lean and water starts sloshing all over us and, more importantly, the dogs. They will never take shelter below, even when walls of green water are soaking them as they shiver in the cockpit. *South Islander* lacks such comfortable cruising aids as a dodger, so my preferred position while in rough seas or inclement weather is sitting on top of the cooler with the hatch slid closed. One of the things I have from my years as a racer is a really good set of raingear. I have very generously given my gear to Tomas so that he can stay relatively dry while at the helm. Never let it be said that I don't have the best interests of my skipper at heart!

Anyway, in 2001 I was still a pretty keen sailor, and *Papillon* was the boat of my dreams. We had decided to stay put at Egmont for a couple of days as the weather was awful – high winds and pouring rain. I would then have the opportunity to ogle *Papillon* every time we passed her on the dock. We only had time for a short, ten-day cruise as we were heading off to Europe to visit family, and the Sunshine Coast (not so aptly named that year) was as far as we planned to go. Egmont is the place where boaters wait for slack before negotiating Sechelt Rapids unless, of course, you do as Tomas did, and wait for "a bit of current to help you through". Conversely people wait for maximum flood or ebb and walk to the Rapids to see this amazing natural phenomenon, touted in tourist info as "the strongest salt water rapids in North America".

We checked the current tables and walked along the beautiful forest trail to the lookout spot. That day it was running 12 or 13 knots, enough to put on quite a show. I couldn't even imagine running a boat through there; it was boiling mass of standing waves and whirlpools. And right in the middle of this maelstrom, were a group of kayakers. But these weren't your regular type of sea kayaks. These resembled fragile plastic shells, barely long enough to accommodate the paddlers' legs. They were cavorting in the rapids, going backwards and forwards and surfing down the waves before climbing back up and doing it all over again. I couldn't believe it – this was the ultimate extreme sport, not to be attempted by any than the most foolhardy. The ground literally shook with the force of the current and I clung to the dogs lest one of them slipped on the moss and was lost over the edge.

Returning to the boat, we left Egmont, heading through Agnew Passage and round the north end of Nelson Island, through Telescope Passage and into the beautiful anchorage at Musket Island. This is not prime territory for dog walks, but there is an island that suffices for the bare necessity of toiletry needs. The little island has a lookout spot where one can look over Malaspina Strait to Texada Island. That day it was whipping the strait up into whitecaps and we were happy to batten down the hatches and crack open the pack of cards.

A little note here on how our boat activities have changed over the years. Before we had laptop computers with DVD drives, our pastimes were limited to reading and games. I often think that the advent of watching movies on the computer has spoiled us for some of the simpler boat pleasures. In the first few years on the boat, I read aloud to Tomas several of the Arthur Ransome books. Those books have endured for 80 years, and although some people, namely my kids, may accuse me of arrested development for reading children's stories, these books perfectly encapsulate the spirit of boating and exploring. Tomas loves them as much as I do. We also played backgammon and cards. I was pretty handy at Racing Demon and Tomas was the Canasta champion. Nowadays we tend to hook up the computer through a complicated system of cords, adaptors and converters and watch movies in bed. I'm not sure Arthur Ransome would have approved.

Something that has not changed over the years is the number of books I read over the course of a summer cruise. I tend to bend my own rules about the quality of books I choose; it's ok to read an occasional bodice ripper – something I wouldn't be caught dead reading at home. One of the cool things about cruising is that at almost every stop you will find a book exchange, be it at a government dock, marine park with a shelter, or even sometimes just a covered shelf along an island trail. I start the summer with a couple of books I don't mind losing, and from there I never have to buy another. The books you can pick up are not always tatty old paperbacks. I've found good-quality hard cover books, normally sold for $40. Just recently I picked up a trade paperback, list price of $19.95, in which I found the receipt. Someone had purchased it just a week before, presumably read it, and then dropped it off at the community notice board of De Courcy Island.

I read, and I read and I read some more. I like to change location, depending on the weather. My very favourite spot on a calm and sunny day is lounging in my hammock, comfortably propped up on pillows and swaying gently as we motor on our way. This only works in very calm conditions, as when the water starts kicking up a few waves, or when we cross another boat's wake, the hammock sets up a wild swinging which threatens to tip me over the side. The final touch is to have a nice cup of tea at hand, or depending on the time of day, a gin and tonic or, our summer favourite, Pimm's.

Let me enlighten you about Pimm's – a secret blend of gin and herbs and spices. This is a traditional English summer drink, usually mixed with 7-Up. The final touch is a slice of cucumber or lemon and a mint leaf; the mint usually omitted when we are on the boat. It is the perfect summer drink, redolent of summer days lazing in a deck chair as the butler hands round the tray of drinks. Not that I've ever been served in a deck chair by a butler, but you get the idea. Actually, Tomas is the perfect boat butler and will serve me Pimm's as I loll in my hammock.

I don't want to give anyone the mistaken impression that Tomas and I are a couple of boozy boaters. As everyone knows, alcohol and boating don't mix. The best time to enjoy a drink is when we are settled into our overnight anchorage, the dogs are relaxing after their shore excursion, and we are just beginning to think about dinner. There is simply no better place on earth to sit and sip, while taking in the incomparable scenery of coastal British Columbia. I've heard it said that our cruising waters are the second best in the world, after the Caribbean. I'm just not buying that. I have seen the pictures of crystal clear waters, white sand beaches and coral reefs. But except for the coral reefs we actually have it all, plus incredible vistas of snow capped mountains and endlessly changing scenery. Don't you think that all those white sand beaches would get boring after a while?

In fact, we have lots of white sand beaches of our own. Savary Island and Thormonby Islands are two examples. I cannot believe that there are beaches any more spectacular anywhere than those surrounding Savary. This island has a reputation for its warm waters and sunny climate. Strangely, in all the years we have been going there, we can only remember it raining once, and that was only a quick shower before the sun came out again. The beaches almost completely encircle the island. Those on the south side have a variety of driftwood shelters, presumably built for shade. That is where I relax with a book while Tomas, who denies the correlation between sun and skin cancer, cooks on the hot sand. It is hard to believe that we are in the same province that delivers months of unending rain during the winter.

Savary has an interesting history, well documented in the book "Sunny, Sandy, Savary". Briefly, it was subdivided at the turn of the century into quarter acre lots, and when I first visited the island in the early 1990s most of the development was on the waterfront lots. Between 1998 and 2009, the change has been dramatic, and not for the good. A vehicle used to be an occasional phenomenon; now cars and trucks constantly travel, often at considerable speed, along the one main road. There are no building schemes, so anything goes in terms of the homes that are being built. And there certainly are some ugly houses. The inland lots are now being developed, and there is a constant whirr of generators and power tools. Still, the beaches remain unspoiled and the back lanes are perfect for cycling.

Tomas and I have a deal. He likes to lie on the beach, I like to cycle the trails. We take turns and rent bikes every second year. On bike years, in addition to the bikes, we also rent a trailer designed to carry children. The dogs reluctantly ride in style, allowed out on the quiet side roads to run alongside.

We, like many other boaters, are very budget conscious. I'm not including "mega-yachts" in this category, as obviously a boat that needs $2,000 worth of fuel to cover the same distance that costs us $200 doesn't have the same budget constraints as we do. This means that more often than not we anchor, rather than mooring at a marina or even tying to a park buoy. Anchoring is one of the great freebies of boating. The sea bottom belongs to us all; anything below the high tide line is public, despite some signage on certain islands that might suggest otherwise. We have heard stories of hapless boaters attempting to stretch their legs ashore only to be met by gun-toting caretakers. I digress.

Anchoring – here's how it's done, or at least here is how we do it. We mosey into a cove and scout out a spot. Tomas lies on the foredeck and unfastens the anchor from its housing under the bow. He lets go. I stand at the helm and follow his directions, which is one of the few times I actually do as I'm told. We reverse slowly as he lets out the anchor rode. He stands with a contemplative look on his face as he scans our position, occasionally tugging on the rode. Eventually he signals me to put the engine in neutral, and finally gestures with a cutthroat motion to kill the motor. We're stuck, and mostly that's the way we stay. We have dragged a few times, but Tomas really is a master of the art of anchoring. He constantly checks the anchor rode, consults the tide tables and the depth sounder, and watches how the boat is swinging. When we leave the boat to take the dogs ashore, we will usually circle the boat a couple of times to check that all is well. Many boaters do not follow these simple precautions and many is the time we've seen a snazzy motor yacht pull into a cove, hurl the anchor over, pay out a bit of line and dive for their dinghy, full speed ahead to the pub. They're the ones who drag anchor.

Now, raising the anchor. We have a splendid, reconditioned winch mounted proudly on the foredeck. Tomas, however, eschews this piece of modern technology and prefers to haul up the anchor hand over hand, foot by foot, like a 17th century tarry sailor on a windjammer hauling on a line as the ship rounds Cape Horn. Either this repeated action has kept his back in relatively good shape, or every time he raises the anchor he is one step closer to a total back failure that will render him crippled. The winch's function, meanwhile, is akin to that of a classy and expensive hood ornament.

That's how we do it. The "mega-yachters", or even some of those on relatively modest boats, have a slightly different technique. The skipper, usually a man of retiree age, nattily attired in blindingly white calf length socks, yachting shoes and cap and jacket monogrammed with the boat's name, stands on the foredeck, often with a two-way radio to talk to the person at the helm, usually The Wife. He then leans forward and presses a button. The anchor lowers and raises with no effort whatsoever, and The Wife follows the radioed directions as to direction and speed. Kind of takes the fun out of it, don't you think?

On occasion we will break down and shell out for moorage at one of the many marinas that dot the coast. Our favourites are the well-run government docks, some of which have facilities better than the private marinas at a fraction of the cost. The only downside is that you usually have to raft up, or be rafted up to. But this is not always a negative as you can meet some interesting people when you are snugged up hull to hull.

So, 2001 wrapped up, and we swathed the boat in her all-enveloping boat cover before heading off to Europe. She would sit happily on her new floating dock, a huge improvement on the old mooring buoy from which she had had her "near death" experience a couple of years before. And here's another of *South Islander*'s endearing traits. Despite having a few strategic leaks, which can be easily managed with carefully rigged tarps, she remains amazingly dry during a long winter sojourn, even without a heater. While other boats sprout mold and drip condensation, *South Islander* breathes like a living being, and greets us in the spring ready for another season of boating.

Chapter Five

2002: CROSSING THE PACIFIC - OR NOT

2002 was the year we acquired Otto. I have previously written about the lo-tech nature of *South Islander*, and our superior attitude towards boaters who have countless gadgets but are often so busy consulting them that they fail to take the simple precaution of looking out of the window.

Many is the time we have observed a boat approaching, usually of the gleaming white variety, and usually travelling at high speed, but with no one visible on the bridge. If we are the "give way" vessel, well, we'll give way, change course, and carry on. If, however, we are the "stand on" vessel, then begins a game of chicken. Why should we change course, when the rules say that they must? Being pretty well educated and experienced boaters, and having had years of Coast Guard Auxiliary training, we are extremely well versed in the rules of the road. It would be nice to think that anyone taking a large and powerful boat out on the open water had at least a modicum of training, but sadly that is not always the case. The most basic rule is to maintain a lookout at all times, even if you have radar, GPS, and an auto helm. So here we are, proceeding on our course, with the right of way over the other boat and they show no sign of altering course. The potential disaster is compounded by the fact that we are going 5 knots and they are going 25 and bearing down on us at alarming speed. The other thing is that you never know what unpredictable move they are going to make as they casually glance out of the window – after having mixed themselves a cocktail in the galley – and see a small wooden sailboat filling their windshield.

Our ploy at this time is to bring out our little air horn and blow it over the side in their general direction. Of course, if the skipper is below there's not much chance of him hearing it. The dogs hate it, and start yowling and barking. I grab the logbook, being the only thing besides

Tomas and the dogs that I figure is worth saving if we have to abandon ship. Fortunately, we've always been able to alter course at the last minute, or the other boat has finally realized that they are on a collision course and swerved to avoid us. I'm sure the skipper of the other boat then has to head below for another stiff drink to bolster his shattered nerves.

In 2009 the graduated scheme for boaters to acquire a Pleasure Craft Operators Card finally included all boaters, regardless of age. Not a moment too soon, in my opinion. The number of "idiot boaters" out there is staggering.

Anyway, back to Otto. Otto is an auto helm, a wonderful electronic gadget that affixes to the tiller and keeps the boat on course. I couldn't understand why we needed one. After all, Tomas was perfectly happy to stand at the tiller in all weather – wasn't he? And we already had an auto helm of sorts. It was a clever combination of bungee cords which, when rigged in a certain way, kept the boat more or less on course. Bungee cords, $5; auto helm, $1,000. What were we thinking? Unlike those idiot boaters we still had to keep watch, so what was the point? OK, I get it now. Instead of standing out in all weathers hanging on to the tiller, Tomas could sit in the hatch, or on the foredeck and effectively keep watch. Otto the Auto Helm really is the most wonderful complement to our boating experience.

We bought Otto #1 in a marine store in Nanaimo at the beginning of our 2002 cruise, and Tomas spend several hours installing it before we headed up to Desolation Sound. We had to calibrate the compass on the device, which involved going round and round in circles – don't ask me to explain that one. Once we had done that, we could set a course and away we went with Otto at the helm. Unfortunately, our delight in our new gadget was short lived as after only a few days Otto quit working. The marine store was very helpful when we called them and agreed to arrange for a new auto helm to be shipped to us, wherever we could be with road access. It took about five days, during which time there were endless updates on shipping progress, and many changes in its eventual destination – Lund, no Egmont, no Lund again, or will we be in Powell River by then, ok, back to Lund. Eventually we picked up Otto #2 in Lund, got it installed, and it has worked like a charm ever since.

At that time we still had neither GPS nor radar. In fact we still don't have radar. We have a huge number of paper charts, including those for crossing the Pacific, and charts of the Hawaiian Islands and South Sea Islands. You see, Tomas built *South Islander* with the plan of sailing her round the world. I think now is the appropriate time to tell you the story of Tomas's attempt to cross the Pacific.

It was 1981, and Tomas and two of his buddies decided that they were going to sail to Hawaii. Never mind that it was November and the start of the winter storm season; they were determined that it was now or never. So they outfitted the boat, crammed her with supplies, and with only a very basic radio that received over short distances but didn't transmit at all, a RDF (Radio Direction Finder) and a compass, they sailed out of Juan de Fuca Strait and into the open Pacific Ocean. They were about three or four days offshore when the storm struck. It was later billed as the Storm of the Century and was in fact a hurricane. *South Islander* plunged onwards through terrific seas as high as her mast with winds they estimated at over 90 knots, until she reached the eye of the storm. Tomas describes it as an unearthly and eerie calm where, all of a sudden, instead of howling winds and driving rain there was no wind and the stars shone down on them through a hole in the clouds. Then all hell broke loose again as they passed the eye and were back in the thick of the storm.

At some point they achieved the near impossible task of turning around and heading back to the West Coast. It was during their return journey, still in the grip of awesome wind and wave, that a freighter loomed out of the night and almost ran them down. The freighter came so close that the sail was blackened by diesel exhaust. No one saw them and it is very easy to see how small boats can be run down in this way with the crew of the freighter unaware of what they have done. It was a very, very near miss and by this time Tomas's crew was ready to jump ship and never set foot on board a boat again.

As they approached the West Coast another danger emerged. Thick fog descended, and having no GPS they really had no idea how close the shore was. It's not called the Graveyard of the Pacific for nothing. It is a cruel and unforgiving shore with very few safe harbours. Eventually, the fog lifted momentarily and Tomas was able to get a fix on Nootka Cone and set a course for Ucluelet. Meantime, his girlfriend at the time had reported to the Coast Guard that he and his buddies were somewhere in the Pacific in the middle of a hurricane. No one held out much hope that they would be found alive, or even at all. As they neared the coast, a Coast Guard vessel on patrol spotted them and led them into Ucluelet. His two crew leapt ashore and Tomas eventually brought the boat solo back to Victoria. And that's the first and last time he or the boat has been further offshore than the middle of Georgia Strait. But what this experience showed him was that he had built *South Islander* strong enough to withstand the most extreme weather conditions. She has never leaked a drop, at least from the bottom up. This is a very comforting thought. Tomas no longer has any desire to sail round the world, which is perhaps just as well as I refuse to go anywhere that is more than a day or so from a pub and a shower!

Despite my love of boating, the open ocean holds absolutely no appeal for me. I just don't understand the desire to spend days on end in the middle of an endless circle of water, braving storms, dodging freighters and scanning the horizon for the first sight of land. It's lucky I ended up living in B.C. where one can sail for years and years and still come across new places. The nearest I ever come to crossing an ocean is when we traverse Georgia Strait, which we do at some point every year. As one shore fades, the other side heaves into view and it's one of the few times we actually sail, since the wind, should there be any, always blows either up or down the Strait, allowing us to reach across. Given the choice, however, I'm sure Moby and Roz would opt for a nice, steady, luxurious motor cruiser, preferably with stabilizers and a companionway they could negotiate unaided.

In 2002 we visited Grace Harbour for the first time, which was strange, as we had passed the entrance to the harbour in 1998 when we had gone into Theodosia Inlet. I think that sub-consciously we were rationing our "discoveries" of all the beautiful anchorages on the coast, and adding a couple of new favourites each year. Grace Harbour is gorgeous, totally protected, with a pleasant walk to a nearby lake, and logging artefacts hidden in the bush. You find these discarded pieces of machinery up and down the coast, and they are evidence of the tremendous tenacity and back-slogging work of the old-time loggers. Grace Harbour is completely inaccessible by road, and the work involved in getting the lumber to market must have been tremendous. As in many old logged-out areas, one sees the stumps of giant trees with the cuts for the springboard and imagines those men ten feet up a tree sawing through enormous trunks with a cross-cut saw. Then having cut down some behemoth without the aid of power tools, they had to get it out of the woods and into the salt chuck so that it could be added to a log boom and taken to the nearest mill, usually many miles away.

In our boat library is one of the *Raincoast Chronicles*, in which you can find amazing tales of the incredible back-breaking and dangerous job of those pioneer loggers. Of course, they had no notion of sustainable logging practices and thought the supply of timber was inexhaustible, but that's another story. What is so amazing is the sheer volume of lumber those early loggers were able to fell with only the most basic of tools. As time progressed, mechanization began to be used and it is often the remains of those early machines that one can find buried in the bush. It seems that when some remote area was logged off, it was simpler just to abandon the machinery than go to the effort and expense of removing it. You can see whole steam engines, drums with loops of curling cable snaking off into the bush, huge pulleys, and pieces that even to Tomas, the ex-logger, are a mystery.

While Tomas was constructing *South Islander* and needed money for materials, he had quickly realized the potential for making large sums in a relatively short time by working as a logger. Of course it's not quite as simple as that, and he tells some pretty funny tales of his early days in the logging camps. He had to work his way up through the lesser and more menial jobs, watching and learning from the old-timers. Eventually, he graduated to being a bona fide "tree murderer", with an enormous chain saw, extremely unfashionable footwear, and a high level of motivation to earn big bucks. On the plus side, he also spent considerable time tree planting, another way that those with energy and endurance can earn a lot of money.

These days Tomas is as environmentally conscious as anyone and deplores the tactics of some of the big logging companies. However, when a tree on our property needs felling, he rubs his hands, oils up the chain saw, puts on his red suspenders and goes to work.

When Tomas first acquired the property it was dense second-growth forest, and chopping down trees was necessary in order to clear a house site. I wince at felling any of the remaining trees, but Tomas knows his stuff and by cutting down some of the smaller ones, the bigger ones grow better. We have some enormous trees on the property, one of which is regularly visited by a couple of eagles. Coming from England it still seems incredibly exotic to have eagles perched in a tree, looking down on our house.

So our 2002 cruise wound to a close, with our last night spent, as it often is, at Conover Cove on Wallace Island. Wallace Island gets a star rating for the quality of its dog walks, and that year we did the long walk to Chivers Point and back. The dogs seemed to realize that our holiday was almost at an end and took full advantage of the interesting smells, weaving in and out of the dense salal as the trail wound through the forest. On the way back we stopped at the old resort where the remains of several cabins and a dining hall are a reminder of the days when the Island was a bustling resort.

David Conover bought the island for $20,000 in 1946. He and his wife were from Los Angeles, and as a young photographer David had photographed Marilyn Monroe when she was still Norma Jeane. Legend has it that Marilyn Monroe visited Wallace Island as a guest of David Conover, but the truth is that Conover never capitalized on this Los Angeles connection and the resort was never a huge success, closing in the 1960s. The old dining hall now has a fascinating display of driftwood boat signs created by passing boaters and hung on the beams.

The next day we left Wallace Island and motored down Trincomali Channel back to Long Harbour and the end of another perfect cruise. At the end of each summer we always vow to do some winter sailing. In reality, apart from a couple of day sails during the fall, the boat has a nice long rest on her dock, no doubt spending those winter nights dreaming of next summer.

Chapter Six

2003: The Year of the Crab or
400 miles and Counting

Remember when I said that Tomas could fix anything? Well, we started our 2003 cruise with the cutlass-bearing going as we motored into Pender Harbour. We had spent the afternoon frolicking on the beach at Buccaneer Bay, and as we entered Pender Harbour the engine started chuntering and clunking. We limped over to the dock at Madeira Park where Tomas gave an instant, and as it turned out, correct diagnosis of "cutlass-bearing gone". Now, if someone had asked me what a cutlass-bearing was, I couldn't even have made an educated guess, so I was immensely impressed by this instant assessment of the problem. In any case we weren't going any further without a repair.

My first move would have been to call a marine mechanic, at which point I would have had to mortgage my house and sell my first born to pay for the repair. However, Tomas is never ever daunted by the prospect of a complicated repair. Rather, he just rolls up his sleeves and gets on with the job.

Fortunately, he had a spare bearing on board. Apparently one must always keep a spare of essential parts; and I thought all those lockers were for food! With this need to have the parts on hand to cover every eventuality, we have a veritable marine parts store on board. Our friends, Keith and Dorothy, towed us over to Whiskey Slough where there is a grid, and once again *South Islander's* twin keels came in handy. We merely towed her up on the grid and tied her to the dock, not having to worry about her tipping over when the tide receded.

There is a brief entry in the logbook – "Tomas (with Keith helping) fixed boat." If only it had been that simple. In reality, changing the bearing involved removing a stubborn coupling in order to extract the propeller shaft. This required a special tool (called a puller), which must be the only tool we don't have on board. However, a friendly nearby boater had one and they finally got the coupling out and the new bearing installed.

We were free to continue our summer cruise, which this year we were doing in convoy with friends. Keith and Dorothy are an interesting couple. Keith made his fortune in the .com business, and in fact their first boat was cleverly named *Dot Calm*. They had moved to Salt Spring from Calgary with absolutely no boating experience, but decided boating looked like fun. *Dot Calm* was only a 23-foot motorboat yet one of the first things they did was install bow thrusters – a piece of equipment wholly necessary if you are a large ferry, but completely unnecessary in a boat this size. *Dot Calm* could now do doughnuts in a space the size of an average garden pond. This will give you an idea of how enthusiastically Keith embraced the whole business of boating. If there was a gadget that he read about or saw in a marine store, and which he thought would enhance his boating experience, well, he got it.

Very soon they decided to trade in *Dot Calm* for a sailing boat, and they bought a modest 27-foot sail boat that they christened *Winter Beater*. Apparently that is a name given to clunker cars that people drive during Alberta winters so as not to wreck their regular vehicles. She was actually the perfect boat for them to learn on, and learn they did. Keith took every boating course available. He is probably the most educated boater I know. But of course theoretical knowledge is no substitute for actually getting out on the water.

While we regularly consult our charts, and take all sensible precautions to ensure a safe boating experience, Keith will approach every day out on the water as if he is preparing for a solo crossing of the Pacific. Charts, tide tables, cruising books, weather forecast will all be assiduously researched, and only after inputting all the relevant data into his computer, firing up the GPS, radar, depth sounder and radio and donning all appropriate safety gear, will he set sail. Very sensible – too bad all boaters aren't as conscientious.

It was a new experience for us to cruise along with friends. Even though we treasure our time on the boat alone with the dogs, it really was fun to have company. It was with some pride that we shared some of our favourite anchorages with "rookies", and we did things we had never done before. I think this was the first time we watched a movie on a laptop computer – Keith always has the most up to date computer gadgets. It was certainly the first (and last) time we ever rented motor scooters. We were in Gorge Harbour and we spent a wonderful day exploring Cortez Island by scooter. The dogs spent some down time lounging on the boat, and it was with very reproachful looks that they watched us paddle ashore without them.

2003 was the Year Of The Crab! After our negative experience losing our brand new crab trap in Evans Bay, it had taken us a while to get round to purchasing a new one. We had dropped it hopefully a few times, but no luck. Someone had told us that crabs prefer cat food to the traditional bait of a turkey leg, so we placed a cracked open tin of cat food inside the trap and dropped it in Waiatt Bay on Cortez Island. This bay is adjacent to the beautiful Octopus Islands Marine Park, which we had approached through the formidable Hole in the Wall (prudently traversed at exactly slack water). Hole in the Wall is a narrow channel separating Sonora and

Maurelle Islands. Approached from the east from Calm Channel it appears wide and devoid of current, but it narrows to a tiny portal at the Okisollo Channel end, and at maximum flood or ebb is a roaring torrent that should only be negotiated at slack water. The Octopus Islands are an incredibly scenic collection of small islands, totally protected from prevailing winds, with a number of snug anchorages and plenty of room for a considerable number of boats. However it is never particularly crowded, probably because the only way to get there is to transit either Hole in the Wall, Surge Narrows, or Okisollo Rapids. Apparently I'm not the only one to view these natural barriers with some trepidation. The park's islands are perfect for short doggie walks ashore and the surrounding scenery is spectacular.

I always find it incredible how uninhabited the West Coast really is. The Octopus Islands are situated at the north end of Quadra Island, and that part of the island is virtually devoid of human habitation. The southern end is where most of the residents live, including an old friend, who lives near Heriot Bay. We visit her most years and one year she drove us up the island to drop off her son who was working as a kayak guide at an isolated lodge. As we drove back towards Heriot Bay in the dusk, she suddenly braked as a huge wolf sauntered across the road in front of us. I couldn't believe my eyes! It just reinforced the fact that here in B.C. we really do live on the edge of the wilderness. Actually it turns out that the wolves will, in fact, venture down towards the southern end of the island, and have been known to take sheep or goats. I was used to coyotes, having lived in the interior of B.C. for many years, but wolves really do seem to epitomise the fact that huge portions of the province still remain largely uninhabited except by our native wild animals. As the wolf loped off into the bush, I clutched Moby to my bosom. Imagine if he had leapt out of the open window and challenged the wolf! A swift end would no doubt have ensued.

The next morning, after a quiet night anchored near one of the tiny islands, we dinghied out to check the trap. To our immense gratification we found an enormous crustacean staring sullenly at us from inside! We kept the fellow alive in a bucket of water and headed through Okisollo Rapids to Thurston Bay Marine Park, a quiet and tranquil anchorage located on the north side of Sonora Island. Once again we found evidence of an abandoned farmstead. What were these people thinking? In an age where there was lots of undeveloped land relatively close to at least of modicum of civilization, these folks set off into the total and absolute wilderness and hacked clearings out of virgin forest. Their Herculean efforts, without the benefit of any power tools and, in most cases without draft animals, are evident in the orchards, irrigation systems and the crumbled remains of buildings. In our travels we have come across dozens of such places, and given that we certainly haven't been into every bay and inlet on the coast, my guess is that there must be hundreds of them.

Some of those early settlers came from very privileged backgrounds. Some left lives where they lived in huge houses with dozens of servants and a pampered lifestyle with no necessity of working for a living. They travelled half way round the world and ended up in some remote spot on the B.C. coast where they exchanged a life of ease for one of extreme labour and hardship. Why did they do it?

Nowadays it would be a noteworthy news story (or perhaps a reality show) if someone set off into totally unexplored wilderness to do what many of these early settlers did. They were obviously made of sterner stuff than we are today. Of course, even these days there are still lots of intrepid explorers, but they eventually fetch up back home and settle themselves comfortably in front of their computers to write their stories. Most of these early pioneers fully intended to spend the rest of their lives living primitive and isolated existences. Many of them lasted only a few years and then headed back to civilization, but there are certainly examples of those who stuck it out. The residents of Port Neville, mentioned in an earlier chapter, are an example of a family that stayed the course. Our coast is a living museum where we can get a glimpse of the lives these people lived. One thing one cannot argue with is the amazing beauty surrounding these abandoned homes. Of course they would have been far, far too busy enduring backbreaking labour to enjoy the luxury of admiring the scenery.

Back to the crab. As we had pulled into the bay, we passed a departing boat that hailed us with a warning. They had seen a very large black bear on the beach that I had just scoped out as a possible dog walk. Those pesky wild animals! However we found a beautiful island in the middle of the bay that was a perfect place to land the dogs. After exploring the old homestead, we humanely despatched the crab and settled down in the cockpit for a gourmet dinner of crab liberally doused in butter and garlic.

That was the first and last crab we have ever caught. Our crab trap has rusted away, and we have been procrastinating about investing in a new one. After eyeing new traps in the marine store and totting up the cost of the one that currently resides on the floor of Evans Bay as well as the one that rust has rendered unusable, we realize that one could enjoy several great crab dinners in an upscale waterfront restaurant for what we have already spent on crabbing equipment.

We left Thurston Bay the next day and started heading back south by transiting Dent Rapids and spending the night in Big Bay on Stuart Island. We passed the entrance to Hole in the Wall, thus making a complete circumnavigation of Sonora Island, and decided to transit Whiterock Passage. This cut runs between Maurelle and Read Islands and has very little tidal flow. It is an alternate route to Surge Narrows and Hole in the Wall, but there's a catch. It is a very narrow passage edged with kelp beds, and with some tricky turns one has to negotiate to avoid running aground. This was the first time we had gone this route, and I immediately thought of Arthur Ransome. In his books there are numerous mentions of "leading lights" and "leading markers", which in today's parlance are called "range markers". It's really quite simple and fun. After carefully studying the chart you set off and look for the two diamond shaped markers on shore with lines through them. One is set above and behind the other and the trick is to line up the lines. Then you know you are on course. At a certain point in Whiterock Passage, when the chart indicates you are approaching the point at which you need to change course, you start looking behind you for the other set of markers. When you get those ones lined up, you change course and keep them in line until you reach the end of the channel.

One of Arthur Ransome's characters is a girl, known in the stories as Captain Nancy. It is she who often instigates and takes charge of the adventures. When one realizes that these books were written barely ten years after women got the vote, it is noteworthy that Ransome chose to portray such a strong female character. In the books she is well versed in navigation and I felt very "Captain Nancyish", as I kept my eye on the markers, whilst observing the kelp beds mere feet away.

Once through the channel, we headed in to the dock at Surge Narrows, which is located on the other side of Read Island from where we had lost the crab trap a few years earlier. There is plenty of current there as it is very close to Beazley Passage and Surge Narrows. As we approached the dock, the dogs starting pacing the deck, anticipating their shore leave. We were about 4 feet away, when I noticed that Moby was about to make an unauthorized leap ashore. At the same moment the boat started to swing away from the dock, caught in the swirling current. As Moby's paws left the deck, I yelled "NO". Time slowed and I watched in horror as he hesitated mid flight, landing in the water between dock and boat. It was a terrifying moment. The current caught him and he was being swept away when my frantic screams caught the attention of a man standing on the dock. With commendable speed he leaned over the dock, grabbed Moby by the handle on his life jacket and hauled him ashore. Poor Moby, he shook and quivered for hours, and has never since taken the liberty of jumping from the boat without a signed release!

Although the dogs are not terribly keen on the big boat, especially in rough weather, they love the dinghy if only because it signifies the end of a sea voyage and the beginning of an exploration ashore. However it has only been in the last few years that they have developed a very amusing habit with regard to the dinghy. What makes this habit even stranger is that Moby has always displayed a marked reluctance to getting his feet wet. While Roz will fetch a stick thrown from shore, Moby considers this game beneath his dignity. He will stand on the shore watching Roz intently as she swims, sometimes for a considerable distance, retrieving the stick. As she approaches the shore, Moby will grab the stick, attempting to keep his feet out of the water, and make off with it as if he'd done the retrieving. And so the game repeats itself as long as we are willing to throw the stick.

When it comes to going ashore, in the early days the dogs would judge the distance from the dinghy to the shore as we approached a beach, and jump only when they were sure they could span the distance. Then one day, as the dogs perched with all four paws on the bow tube, Tomas quickly back paddled which caused the dogs to fall into a few inches of water just short of the beach. And that was the beginning of the game. Nowadays, despite the fact that Moby will never enter the water willingly from shore, he will eagerly leap from the dinghy and swim to shore, over ever-increasing distances. The game now goes as follows: we board the dinghy from the boat and head towards shore; the dogs start quivering with anticipation and I keep a firm hold on them until I feel comfortable with the distance remaining to shore. Then I let go and they leap out of the dinghy and swim ashore. The leap itself is something to behold. Jack Russells are known for their jumping ability and they make good use of this inherent talent by jumping up off the tube, forward through the air with their feet tucked under them in a streamlined flying position, and then splashing down to start the long swim ashore. Anyone nearby is treated to a very amusing spectacle and many is the time we've seen fellow boaters in paroxysms of mirth at the sight of our two "flying" Jack Russells. What makes it so odd is that after reaching shore Moby displays no further interest whatsoever in swimming or even getting his paws wet.

2003 must take the record for one of the hottest summers we have ever spent on the boat. I keep weather records and out of 23 days only one has been recorded as "cloudy". Of the remaining 22 days, 10 I recorded (somewhat vaguely) as "warm", 7 as "hot", 4 as "very hot", and one as "very, very hot". We really should get a proper thermometer, but I like the anecdotal nature of my weather records. On the days that it was "very hot" or "very, very hot", we could have been in any tropical paradise, except for the absence of palm trees. Even on the moving boat it was almost unbearable, and we resorted to pulling up buckets of water to slosh all over ourselves. On those days, the anchorages that boasted nearby lakes drew us like magnets, and we stopped at every one we could.

That extremely hot summer was the year of the terrible forest fires up in the Okanagan. One night, while we were anchored at Newcastle Island, I had a most peculiar dream about my good friend Molly (the same Molly who has illustrated this book), who at that time lived in Armstrong. In the dream she and I were leading two of her horses down a tunnel to escape a forest fire. At the end of the tunnel we emerged to find that the fire had been extinguished by a snowfall. The next day a friend called to tell me that Molly had been evacuated from her farm and had had to move the horses to safety. Never, before or since, have I have had a dream that predicted reality in such a dramatic fashion. I have always denied any belief in premonitions or anything psychic or "new agey". I attribute this brief encounter with ESP with being on the boat, away from the stresses and outside influences of our day-to-day life.

The last night of our cruise was spent in Telegraph Harbour on Thetis Island. During the night the wind started to howl and we began to drag anchor. We almost ended up on a dock, but managed to reset the anchor without doing any damage. The next day we stopped on Wallace Island and walked from Conover to Princess Cove, where we observed a large motor-boat aground. It had also dragged its anchor and ended up wedged between two tiny islands. It took several days and a salvage company to get it off, and it sustained major damage. Did I mention that boating is an expensive business?

We got back to Long Harbour that evening with a strange statistic to record in the logbook. That year we had gone exactly 400 nautical miles. And I don't mean 399.4, of 401.2, I mean precisely 400 miles as measured by our GPS, from the moment we let loose the lines 23 days earlier, to the moment we tied up. I just love keeping the log, if only to have such odd facts to report!

Chapter Seven

2004: THE YEAR THE WHALES HID

2004's boating season began with a near miss from running very hard aground. It was February and not our preferred time of year for boating, but we had some friends from England staying, and they are very, very keen sailors. Notwithstanding a miserable, cold and windy day, we agreed to take them over to Montague Harbour on Galiano Island. The boat had been sitting at the dock all winter without much attention, other than an occasional check on her lines. After months of sitting idle, and with barely a cough, the engine sprang to life with one turn of the key. We motored out of Long Harbour and rounding Nose Point raised the double reefed main sail. Then, with all of us sensibly attired in full floater suits and several layers of fleece we began a very cold reach across Trincomali Channel.

At this point I will reiterate that I am now very much a fair-weather boater. I can think of many things I would rather be doing than sitting cold and damp on a heeling deck, getting liberally splashed with freezing seawater. Fortunately, it's not that far to Montague and I was looking forward to firing up the diesel stove and having a nice cup of tea.

As we approached Phillamore Point, the entrance to Montague, we prepared to tack. All the appropriate orders were sung out smartly in the correct nautical parlance, and Tomas swung the tiller across to change tack. Nothing happened. The boat continued to plough through the waves towards the point. He tried again – nothing. We were now alarmingly close and I started to panic. What had happened? Had we somehow lost our rudder? Time expanded, and what was in fact only seconds seemed like hours. When the point was a mere hundred feet away, Tomas started the motor, dropped the mainsail and managed to manoeuvre the boat round the point. At that juncture it wasn't tea I needed, but a stiff drink! We motored into Montague and tied up to the dock.

The problem proved to be a huge build-up of mussels on the rudder that had impaired the steering. Let that be a lesson: check the relevant moving parts on your boat after a winter of sitting motionless. It's one thing to go a tad slower than usual because of growth on the hull, but it's useful to be able to steer the boat!

That summer we decided to approach our seasonal cruise a bit differently. We wanted to cruise the Broughton Archipelago at the northern end of Vancouver Island. We had not yet made it up there after our aborted attempt in 1999. I was involved in a major theatre production so we decided that Tomas would do a "yacht delivery" while I was doing the show. He would leave the boat in Alert Bay, and we would return in August to start our summer cruise. This meant that without me or the dogs, he could travel much faster and do the trip in 6 days. He invited my son, Adam, and his dad, Rod, to make the trip with him. They had a few hairy moments approaching the dock at Ford Cove on Hornby Island, in the dark and with 25 knots of wind, but otherwise they had a fairly uneventful trip up the coast to Port McNeill, where I drove up to fetch Tomas home. I think Adam found the trip rather boring, as he apparently slept most of the way and leapt onto a Greyhound bus back to Victoria the moment they arrived in Port McNeill.

There was one moment of humour on around Day 3 of the trip, when Husband #1 said to Husband #2 that I mustn't be told that they had eaten their carefully prepared and labelled meals in the wrong order. Am I really that particular? Rhetorical question!

I drove up to fetch Tomas and we had a few days before we had to head back home. We decided to do a mini-cruise, taking in Sointula and Telegraph Cove. For those of you who have not visited this part of the coast, I have one word of advice – go! Anyone who is interested in West Coast history will find they've hit the jackpot. First stop for us was Sointula on Malcolm Island. Finnish immigrants settled the island in the early 1900s and established a "utopian social-ist society", but the community fairly quickly disbanded. However, many of the original immi-grants' descendents still live on the island and it has a quaint old-world feel to it. We tied up in Rough Bay Harbour and walked with the dogs to town where there was a nice coffee shop right on the water. The museum is definitely worth a visit, crammed with fascinating artefacts from the early days.

We anchored in Double Harbour that night and awoke the next day to an impenetrable fog. Our newly acquired GPS, plugged into our laptop, showed us precisely where we were so we decided to go ahead and move over to Telegraph Cove – not a very long trip. There is one catch however, and that is that one has to traverse Johnstone Strait, and Johnstone Strait is the highway for cruise ships heading to Alaska. Take thick fog, large cruise ships and a small wooden sailboat which may be blindly crossing their path and you have a potential disaster in the making. Undaunted, we set off, with me sitting in the companionway with our little foghorn, blasting away at regular intervals. We really were following all the rules, but in retrospect it seems we were a bit foolhardy.

Telegraph Cove is impossibly quaint. The village started life as a salmon saltery and sawmill operation, but now caters solely to the tourists, many of whom come to experience a close encounter with the resident Orca whales. Johnstone Strait is the home to pods of northern resident Orcas, and Telegraph Cove is ideally suited as a base for whale watching and kayak tours. The village is built along a boardwalk, with many of the original buildings converted to tourist accommodations. As well, there is a truly fascinating whale museum. Unfortunately, across the tiny cove from the boardwalk is the biggest, ugliest marina and motel I have ever seen. What possessed the powers to be to give permission for this monstrosity is a complete mystery. I spent most of my first visit there trying not to look at it. The contrast between the gaily-painted cabins and cottages along the boardwalk and the rearing wall of the hotel across the water is horrible to behold.

We decided to leave the boat in Alert Bay on Cormorant Island, in the very splendid government dock. Before heading back over to Port MacNeill to pick up our car and head back to Salt Spring, we took a walk from the village to the Indian Reserve where we had heard there was a museum. The first thing you see is a huge brick building with peeling paint and a general air of neglect. This is home to the band offices, but that's not the interesting thing about this building. The interesting fact is that this is one of the few buildings that remain standing from the residential school days. It was built sometime in the 1920s and one can only imagine the labour involved in transporting the materials for this building all the way from Vancouver. I mean, this is not a frame or log building; it's an enormous multi-storey brick edifice, built for the sole purpose of "educating" native children. It is poetic justice that the native band now has use of the place that so badly used their parents and grandparents.

Right beside the old school, is the U'mista Cultural Centre, built in the form of a traditional longhouse. The end facing the ocean is painted with beautiful native designs and flanked by totems, but it is what the museum houses that is truly fascinating. As well as being a general museum with some very interesting exhibits, the museum has regained their collection of potlatch regalia, and those are incredible to behold. Displayed amongst the stunning masks are copies of letters from the Indian agent and other government officials at the time the regalia was confiscated. It is fascinating to read how these misguided people justified confiscating such beautiful works of art from their rightful owners.

Apart from the museum, Alert Bay is truly a nice place to visit on a boat, particularly if you are travelling with your canine family members. There are lots of places to walk, including an ecological reserve with a boardwalk that meanders through a bog, and a native cemetery complete with some impressive totems which you can observe from the road (entry not permitted).

We felt very confident leaving our boat at the dock and sure enough, when we returned a month later she was just as we had left her, snugly tied and waiting for us to release her from her moorings and start our main summer cruise.

A friend drove us back up to Port MacNeill, and we crossed back to Alert Bay on the ferry. After stocking up on some essentials, such as gin, tonic and lemons, our first stop was Village Island and the deserted native settlement of Mamalilaculla. We walked along the sunlit trail from the dock to the village and were immediately transported to another world. The remains of the longhouse are still evident in some standing poles, but most amazing is the collapsed totem that lies covered in moss among the trees. You can still see the shapes and forms of the stylized animals slowly melding with the earth. I recalled that the native culture expected totems to be impermanent, not preserved as we so often see them in museums. True, the splendid totems in the Anthropological Museum at UBC are a wonder to behold, but somehow this totem in its natural habitat, fallen exactly where it was initially erected, was a far more moving sight.

There are some old European-style houses and a crumbling building that was originally a fever hospital, but the whole settlement is quietly settling into the ground. In a few years there will be very little left to see. Some artefacts will last a little longer, such as the rusting engine and metal boat parts littering the beach, but in a way they make the history more complete; totems representing life before European contact, and the metal litter representing the influence of white man. I wonder what the village would look like if Captain Vancouver had never "discovered" this beautiful land.

We really were on a roll with history and museums and I realized that seeing the artefacts and reading the local history of this part of the coast brought the past vividly to life. By comparison the ancient collections in the British museums I know so well and have visited so often seem remote and inaccessible. And the best was still to come because the next stop was Echo Bay and Billy Proctor's museum. Much has been written about Billy and I will only say that there is a wonderful doggie walk from the head of the bay, past the school house and through the woods to Billy's museum, in which we spent a couple of hours examining his fabulous collection. To get a picture of the history of this part of the coast Billy's museum is an essential stop. And chatting to him brought us a sense of the toughness necessary to survive and make a living on this remote part of the coast.

Since the nominal title of this book is *Memoirs of a Cruising Dog,* and its purpose is to guide boaters with canine companions to good, accessible dog walks, I will say here and now that the Broughton Islands are not the best place in the world to cruise with dogs. Many anchorages have very marginal shore access, and several of the marinas are, in fact, a series of docks bolted to an impenetrable shoreline. They may advertise "dog walk" but sometimes the actuality is a 6-foot square of tattered turf perched on the edge of a float. Pierre's Landing has just such a "dog walk", but was still definitely worth a visit. During the summer months Pierre regularly hosts a pig roast on a large covered portion of the dock. There is also a splendid bakery housed in a reproduction windmill (perhaps the builders were Dutch). Several people live there year round on colourful houseboats, some housing small craft shops. We also stopped in at Sullivan Bay, which is a charming destination, complete with its own jail and signpost to many global destinations, but again nowhere to walk the dogs. One of the permanently moored houseboats had a helicopter perched on its top deck – making the owners' access to this beautiful spot a hop, skip and a jump from civilization, rather than the 10 days it had taken us to get there.

There are, however, a couple of doggie gems in the area. The first we encountered was Cypress Harbour, a beautiful secluded and protected cove with a trail through the woods to a rocky grotto. We moved on that day to Greenway Sound and anchored overnight. Despite the paucity of dog walks at the marina, we discovered a truly wonderful walk to Broughton Lake.

The water was tepid, so we had a leisurely swim and it felt as if we were in some exotic tropical destination rather than coastal British Columbia.

The previous Christmas I had bought Tomas the gear a fishing friend recommended for catching salmon on the West Coast. I was rather afraid that the gear, much like the crab trap, would never reap us a single fish, but the next day we caught our very first salmon. Sadly, patience is not my strong suit, and to fish one has to be patient. The gear is complicated, but Tomas had read several books and studied assiduously before casting the first line. It involves weights, flashing things, strange plastic lures that look like kids' toys, a machine called a downrigger fixed to the stern rail (the platform the downrigger is mounted on took several months of planning and construction) and last, but not least, a fishing rod. I simply don't understand how it's done, and because one has to troll along at a very slow speed, I get impatient after a few minutes of going nowhere fast with no fish fighting to be our supper. Not to mention grumbling under my breath about how much the equipment had cost and calculating that if we ever caught one it was going to work out to about $300 per pound! So it was tremendously exciting when Tomas hooked that first salmon which was landed, humanely despatched, cleaned and put on ice for supper. There was some discussion about its weight, as at that time we didn't have a fish scale. Our estimates differed by about 10 pounds!

I have to say that $300 per pound was cheap for that salmon dinner. If you have never eaten fish straight from the sea you have missed out on an exquisite culinary experience. There must be no finer dinner than fresh salmon cooked in foil on the barbeque with lemon and mayonnaise. It was truly a dinner for the Gods.

One of our stops was in Tracey Harbour. Here was a logging operation that didn't seem to have changed much since Tomas was last there as a young logger, 30 years before. When there is no active logging it is a peaceful spot, totally protected with good access ashore and a network of old logging roads.

So onward and forward to one of our more dramatic experiences on this trip, at least for me with my, as it turned out not unreasonable, fear of wild animals. We left the Broughton Islands behind and, with a brisk wind, sailed down Tribune Channel and into Kwatsi Bay. There is a small marina there run by a young family who had embraced the life of those early settlers. They had hacked and hewn a clearing out of the bush, floated in a cabin, constructed some docks and bingo – a marina! We pulled up to the dock, looking forward to going ashore for a nice long walk with the dogs. We were met by the owner, Max, toting a rifle. Not so friendly a greeting I thought, before he explained the reason for the gun. Apparently there was a marauding cougar in the vicinity that had been circling the house the night before, possibly anticipating one of the couple's young children as a bedtime snack. I paled, clutched the dogs and gave up any thoughts of the walk to the nearby waterfall. Max agreed to escort us ashore, and that's how we "walked" the dogs – tightly restrained on the leash, looking nervously over our shoulders for the cougar while Max stood on guard with his gun loaded and ready. I love telling that story to my family back home in England. That night, tied to the dock, we heard the caterwauling of the cougar, which was prowling for easy prey. I couldn't wait to move on!

Our next stop was Lagoon Cove on Minstrel Island. We had heard about this place, with its daily offering of free shrimp, and we were not disappointed. Bill and Jean come up from the States every summer to run the marina and they have the right attitude essential for those in the hospitality industry, which is that they just love all the visitors. Every evening all the marina guests are invited up to the top of the dock for Happy Hour. Bill catches buckets of shrimp each day, Jean cooks them up, the visitors bring appies and drinks and voila! It was great fun, made even more memorable by the presence of a large, black bear up in one of their fruit trees. Everyone hurried over to observe the animal gorging on ripe fruit. He must be the most photographed bear on the coast, and no doubt his mug shot adorns photo albums across North America. There is also a pleasant trail to walk the dogs, so all in all it is a 5-star stop.

The next few days saw us scooting back south, hoping to catch a sight of some Orcas in Johnstone Strait, but no luck there. In order to squeeze through the rapids that lie approximately midway down Vancouver Island and spit ourselves back into southern waters, we timed our transit through Green Pointe, Dent, Gillard, Yuculta and Hole in the Wall rapids all on one tide. This is possible if you time your voyage carefully. We were back in our familiar territory, with another beautiful evening in the Octopus Islands.

We revisited many of our favourite spots on our way back home and ended our cruise at the Wooden Boat Festival in Vancouver. We made the surprising discovery that it was possible to moor the boat at the Government Dock at Fisherman's Wharf in False Creek. We paid the same at we would at any Government Dock along the coast, but were in the middle of the city with splendid facilities and a short dinghy ride over to Granville Island. It was a novel experience to be staying on our boat in such an urban setting. The festival is a great chance to ooh and aah over fabulously restored wooden boats, including the famous Pardeys' wooden masterpiece, *Taleisin*. The Pardeys eschew such modern conveniences as an engine and have sailed around the world and into many of the busiest harbours on the planet without the benefit of engine power. They are truly exceptional sailors and their books make great reading when we are tamely motoring along in a flat calm.

We crossed over False Creek, beached our dinghy and went for dinner in the West End. Friends invited us for a meal at their house in West Vancouver, and several old friends made special trips down to the boat to visit. It was a surprisingly enjoyable few days, and we saw a city we know well from a totally different perspective.

Crossing Georgia Strait is usually one of the times we are guaranteed to sail, as the wind is either blowing up or down the strait and we can beat or tack. That year was no exception and we had a good sail across and into another of our favourite stops, Silva Bay. The bay is nestled amongst the Flat Top Islands and is nicely protected on all sides. In addition, there is a great pub. It is also possible to dinghy with the dogs over to Drumbeg Park for a pleasant walk on the shoreline trail.

It is traditional to end our summer cruise with a last night at Conover Cove on Wallace Island. We always have a special last dinner, followed by an even more special breakfast. For those of you who have ever stayed in a British bed and breakfast this sort of breakfast is known as the Full English, and in order to qualify for the title all the food, including the bread, is fried in a liberal amount of grease. Replete with a year's worth of cholesterol we motored the last hour and a half back to our dock in Long Harbour and snugged up dear old *South Islander* for the long winter ahead.

Chapter Eight

2005: THE YEAR OF THE HOLDING TANK

With commendable understatement, the log entry for June 3rd, 2005 notes:

"...last few bits and pieces delayed ETD from 0900 to 1430".

I could write an entire chapter on the planning and execution of installing a holding tank, but I will only inflict on you the abbreviated version of the saga. Suffice to say that this was a "big job". We had been intending to do it for years, but the push came when we decided to take a long-awaited trip to the San Juan Islands, and holding tanks are mandatory in the United States. God only knows why they are not so in Canada, but they weren't then and they aren't now. The good old U S of A beat it to us with their marine environmental policies. In any case, we felt it was our duty as responsible boaters to get the job done, and our intended destination across the border gave us the incentive we needed. Tomas, as usual, approached the project with his "can do" attitude, and beetled off to the marine store to purchase the necessary parts. Naively, I thought that all that was needed was the actual tank and a couple of hoses. Not so. The list of parts required was long, and when Tomas actually got down to work it looked as if there had been an explosion aboard, with him sitting in the tiny head in the middle of a mass of nuts, bolts, hoses, clamps and tools.

My squeamishness about the whole project came to a "head" when I realized that the tank itself had to be situated under the bed. Every other location on the boat was suggested, explored and dismissed, and the outcome was that there was only one place to put it. I just had to get over it. Since Tomas is an incurable optimist the job itself took about ten times longer than was estimated, but finally it was done and we could start our season of boating with a clear conscience.

We began by circumnavigating Salt Spring, with stops on Portland Island, Maple Bay and Conover Cove. Portland Island remains one of our all time favourite spots. It has everything – a choice of two lovely anchorages, some of the best doggie walks on the coast, and a fascinating history. Way back at the turn of the century it was settled by Kanakas, immigrants from the Hawaiian Islands, and later owned in the 1920s by an eccentric retired army officer who planned to raise and train thoroughbred racehorses on the island. Almost a hundred years later, one can see the remains of the large cleared area in the middle of the island where there was once a training track. It's hard to imagine the scene back then, with a large barn, bustling activity and the horses whirling round the track. Nowadays, it is a beautiful, tranquil spot, with a wide woodland trail linking the two anchorages, and an easy coastal trail that circles the island.

At the end of June we started our long-awaited San Juan Island cruise. Since 9/11, crossing the border had become such a hassle that we demurred and stayed in Canada. This time, however, we were determined. The customs officer couldn't have been nicer, and greeted us with a potted history of why the San Juan Islands were American, not British. When he noticed my English accent, he even apologized for taking the islands away from us! We had landed at Roche Harbour, which is a very quaint village with many historic buildings. There is an interesting walk to a strange mausoleum in the woods where John S. McMillin, who founded the Roche Harbor Lime and Cement Company, is buried along with his family members. It is a very peculiar structure, apparently based on the Masonic principles in which he believed, but which ends up looking like some odd Greek temple dropped incongruously onto a Pacific Northwest island.

On the suggestion of our friendly customs officer, we headed over to the English Camp at Garrison Bay to anchor for the night. The English Camp was established in 1859 when the so-called Pig War erupted. The Americans and the British (in the guise of the Hudson's Bay Company, which represented Britain's interests at the time) had both claimed the San Juans as part of their territory, but an uneasy peace had prevailed until an American settler killed a pig belonging to a Hudson's Bay settler. Then, to coin a phrase, all hell broke loose and the ensuing dispute lasted 12 years. During that time 461 Americans, hugely outnumbered by 2,140 British and 5 British war ships, were stationed on the island. Each side established a camp, but the English side really got themselves organized by locating their camp in a delightful spot on Garrison Bay, building proper accommodation, laying out gardens and even erecting a bandstand. Life there was very pleasant, with parades, concerts and tea parties. In comparison the American Camp was supposedly built in a bug-infested swamp. However, the Americans had the last laugh as Kaiser Wilhelm of Germany was appointed to settle the dispute and he gave the islands to the Americans.

The Americans, let it be said, do parks very, very well. They have not, like we in British Columbia, contracted out park maintenance to profit-driven companies, resulting in park services being drastically reduced or even eliminated. This is a huge mistake. Other than making a bit of money by providing the bare minimum of service, the Park Facility Operators have no stake in our beautiful parks. The problem is that B.C has made operating the parks a matter of profit for the contractors, and there is no profit in parks. There's not supposed to be. Parks give something intangible to the people that use them, and we are immeasurably better off as a society if we avail ourselves of them. The U.S. park system appears to embrace this philosophy. Their park rangers take enormous pride in job, have a smart uniform and the authority that goes with it and seem to treat the parks as if they were their own domain – it shows!

In addition, they have a great park volunteer program where volunteers, usually seniors, give talks and offer all kinds of information to visitors. Our visit to the English Camp included a marvellous movie and an enthusiastic volunteer sharing all the history we could absorb about the area.

Stuart Island was our next stop, and another wonderful walk with the dogs from Reid Harbour to the lighthouse at Turn Point. Turn Point is so named as it is the spot where the huge freighters turn out of Boundary Pass into Haro Strait, or vice versa. It is apparently quite common to see pods of killer whales right off the point, but we were not so lucky. The lighthouse itself in its magnificent setting is well worth the fairly long walk from the park.

We cruised on over to Friday Harbour, the mecca of the San Juan Islands. Friday Harbour is actually a small town, with historic buildings lining the streets, a vibrant waterfront with green space and cafes and a very well run municipal marina. It is the way I had imagined an island village would be until I moved to Salt Spring Island with its village of Ganges and was sorely disappointed.

It has long been a contentious issue on Salt Spring Island whether or not to incorporate into a municipality, which would mean we would have a mayor and council just like Friday Harbour does. It has always been voted down, with the naysayers frightening everyone with talk of higher taxes. The reality is that we are part of the Capital Regional District, and as such have little say in how our village is run. The example of Salt Spring's unfinished boardwalk is trotted out every time the incorporation issue is raised. The boardwalk was designed to run all the way round the head of Ganges Harbour, from downtown to the pub at the other side of the harbour. It was started almost 30 years ago and has never been finished. Smack dab in the middle is Cudmore's Gap, the result of a dispute between an old-time islander and the Islands Trust. So the boardwalk remains, with stairs leading to nowhere and the part that is finished ending in a rail with a tantalizing glimpse of the other side, more boardwalk, and no way to get there except to climb up onto the road and risk your life dodging traffic on the sidewalkless road.

Friday Harbour has, no doubt, a very efficient mayor and council, and it shows. No unfinished boardwalks here! Flower baskets everywhere. Charming and friendly locals. We explored the town, shopped at the well-stocked grocery store, rented a video and spent the evening snugged up to the dock with a good bottle of wine.

Our next stop was East Sound on Orcas Island. This is not a great anchorage, but we found a good enough spot made possible once more by our shallow draft. The village of East Sound is another San Juan gem, and we had landed there on the July 4th weekend. There was a terrific craft market and a fabulous parade, over flown by a contingent of military jets. I found the contrast between the parade, with its gay and lesbian float sporting rainbow colours and pink balloons, and the militarism of other sections of the parade culminating with the fly by of the jets, very interesting. I think many Canadians have a notion of Americans as being all right wing, gun-toting, anti-gay Republicans. What I saw was a community with great pride in their country, supportive of their military, yet tolerant of those who espoused a different lifestyle. I really liked it here.

After a night in the charming town of La Conner, we had a long motor down the coast of Whidbey Island to Port Townsend - not to be missed if you are a wooden boat aficionado. This is the home of the Port Townsend Wooden Boat Festival, which was not on at that time, but nonetheless there always seem to be lots of boats to gawk at. We often get ideas for improving our own boat by looking at other beautifully crafted and maintained wooden boats.

The town itself is a gem, with dozens of Victorian brick buildings downtown and stately mansions lining the quiet leafy streets above the town. That night we sat on the beach and looked out at the San Juan Islands. It was July 4th and we got an astonishing display of fireworks in not one, but several locations. Our American cousins certainly know how to set off fireworks!

The next day we had one of the most unpleasant voyages I have yet to experience on the boat. There was no wind, but despite that there were enormously steep seas. It was a classic example of wind over tide. There had been a windy night, with the prevailing wind heading our direction, resulting in lumpy swells. The tide was pushing the swells in the other direction, creating short, sharp waves. It was perfectly dreadful. At one point a large green wall of water crashed into the cockpit soaking us and, more to the point, the poor shivering dogs. They positively refused to go below where it was dry and warm, but preferred to suffer in silence, quivering in the bottom of the cockpit. Finally the seas subsided and we ended our voyage back on Stuart Island, but this time in Prevost Harbour, across a neck of land from Reid Harbour.

We awoke the next morning, July 7th, 2005, to the terrible news from London about the Tube and bus bombings. Just as one always remembers where one was at momentous moments in history, so I will always recall awaking to a pristine, calm and stunningly beautiful West Coast morning and hearing about the carnage in London. Only two other world events have evoked those time and place memories, the first being the assassination of JFK when I was ten years old, and of course the other being the more recent events of 9/11.

We ended our first cruise that year by crossing back into Canada and checking in at Bedwell Harbour on Pender Island. No one at Canada Customs seemed much interested in our arrival, and it was all done quickly over the phone before we headed back into Long Harbour.

That year my two sisters, Clare from England and Caroline from Denmark, visited us. One day we decided to have a family picnic at Montague Harbour on Galiano Island. After a delicious meal on the grassy lawn by the north-facing beach we headed back into Trincomali Channel on our way home. Suddenly we heard the unmistakable blow of a whale and, lo and behold, as if on order for our European visitors, a pod of Orcas appeared along the west side of Parker Island. We followed them at a respectable distance for an hour or so, transfixed by the sight of these magnificent creatures in their natural habitat. My sister Caroline's entry in the log book reads:

> "Whales, whales and yet more whales. Makes our 25,000 kroner air fare well
> worth it!"

That was actually the first time I had ever seen Orcas in our local waters. In fact, I'd never ever seen one in the wild before, despite having spent a considerable amount of time out on the water over the previous 15 years. I can only grimace when I hear tales of first-time visitors to B.C. boarding a ferry and being treated to a display of leaping and cavorting whales as they cruise through Active Pass. It's just not fair!

We really did have a plethora of visitors that year. In August my Spottiswoode cousins visited from their home in Los Angeles, and ended their stay by buying a house on Salt Spring. We took them to all our favourites spots, seeing those familiar places with new eyes as they expressed their enthusiasm for the Gulf Islands by swimming across coves, exploring trails we seldom venture on and gasping in astonishment at the wildlife in our back yard. On one trip Natasha notes in the logbook:

"saw 200-odd seals, four porpoises and an eagle".

And that was just on one afternoon!

Our main summer cruise began by not beginning. We had planned to leave at around supper-time and spend our first night back at Conover Cove. However, last-minute jobs kept popping up and by the time we were ready to leave it was almost bedtime. I was not amused at having our departure delayed, so Tomas pacified me by suggesting we sleep on the boat at the dock and leave at first light. First light in August is around 4:30 am, so that's when we left. I stayed in bed with the dogs and Tomas motored us up Trincomali Channel to De Courcy Island in time for breakfast.

It was a beautiful summer day, calm and hot and we headed ashore for a walk with the dogs. Roz has always had a tendency to take off after deer or small animals, but Moby, being the sensitive soul that he is, usually stays pretty close to us on walks. However this time they both disappeared, hurling themselves into the bush after some forest critter. Their barks faded into silence as we called fruitlessly until we were hoarse. After about 20 minutes Roz sheepishly reappeared, but there was no sign of Moby. I was seriously worried. Roz has an amazing ability to find her way back to us, even if we have moved significantly from the spot where she went missing, but Moby's tracking ability had never been put to the test. Eventually we headed back to where we had left the dinghy, envisioning spending our entire holiday searching for him on DeCourcy. As we came out of the woods and down onto the beach, there he was, sitting quivering beside "his" dinghy. There were several tenders on the beach, but Moby knew which one belonged to him. This event must have had a serious psychological affect on him, as from that day to this, he has never been out of sight of us for more than a couple of minutes. Roz, however . . . . ! Now that she is stone deaf, we no longer bother to call her, but she always reappears sooner or later, finding us by who knows what instinct.

That year we again met up with Keith and Dorothy for a joint cruise. By then they had graduated from *Winter Beater*. They were now the proud owners of a gleaming steel yacht they had renamed *Tahi*. When they had decided to trade up, they had consulted us asking us to help them buy a new boat. How much fun can it be spending someone else's money? The answer is – lots! We looked at several boats, but *Tahi* was the one. The boat had been kept in pristine shape by its previous owner, but that didn't stop Keith redoing just about everything on board, including all the rigging, boat cushions and electronics. That boat could have sailed itself around the world!

After a stop at Newcastle Island we headed out to cross Georgia Strait. Now that day, for some inexplicable reason that might have had something to do with the extremely good bottle of wine we had consumed on *Tahi* the night before, we neglected to listen to the marine radio weather forecast which includes notices to mariners, and blithely set our course across the Strait. All of a sudden we noticed a large motorboat bearing down at us. As it came closer, still going full tilt, we heard sirens wailing and saw several men on deck waving frantically. We were under sail and therefore had the right of way, but that boat was just not slowing down or altering course. We hooted our foghorn, frantically gesturing at the crew of the other boat to change course, but it didn't slow down until it was a mere 50 feet from us. It was a terrifying few minutes. As the other boat came alongside we noted that it was flying both Canadian and U.S. flags and that it had a distinctive military look to it. The crew yelled at us that we had wandered into Whiskey Gulf, the area in Georgia Strait which is used for military exercises. They were playing war games that day and we had been in danger of being sunk by a torpedo, or so they led us to believe. After some frantic chart work, we realized that although we were indeed heading for Whiskey Gulf, we were still a couple of miles outside it. We complained to the appropriate authorities about the heavy-handed approach of the military and received an apology. But that incident left me with a few more grey hairs! We have never again strayed within 5 miles of that area and always check very carefully to find out if Whiskey Gulf is "active" on the day we plan to cross Georgia Strait.

That day we stopped in Squitty Bay, and in calm conditions were able to negotiate the entrance which is narrow and rocky. It can be very intimidating when there is any sort of wind as it is on the extreme southern end of Lasqueti Island, and the entrance becomes a mass of breaking waves when the wind is coming from the southeast. Inside it is a cozy harbour with a small government dock and we stopped long enough for lunch and a swim.

We wanted to show Keith and Dorothy another of our favourite spots, Tenedos Bay. So after stopping at Pender Harbour and Lund, we motored into the bay and found ourselves our very own cove away from most of the other boats. Anchoring was a fairly new thing for Keith and Dorothy, as they mainly like to tie up to a marina, but we persuaded them that this was a great place to spend the night so they agreed to give it a try. Their technique was as follows: Keith would stand on the foredeck with a two-way radio, talking to Dorothy in the cockpit at the helm. He would scout out a suitable spot and drop the anchor overboard. Dorothy would then put the engine in reverse and go backwards at full speed as yards and yards of heavy chain came screaming out of the chain locker. Finally, as the anchor grabbed onto the bottom, they would lurch to a stop. They would be stuck, but with about 300 feet of chain lying on the bottom, three times more than they needed in that depth. They had enough chain out to secure the Queen Mary! This was before Keith installed a modern electric winch; the one they had at the time lifted about 3 links of chain for every crank of the winch — no wonder they preferred to tie to a dock.

That night the wind began to blow, and it was decided that *Tahi* was too close to shore. Moving her was a massive undertaking, but finally she was anchored again in a safer spot. Keith stayed up all night monitoring his GPS, which told him to the foot, exactly where he was and if he was dragging. We, as always, slept sound and safe on sweet *South Islander*.

We cruised along with Keith and Dorothy for a few more days before they headed off home and we slowly meandered back down south. One day we had one of the most terrifying experiences we have ever had – strange that over all those years of cruising, we should have two near misses in one season. We were heading south down Sabine Channel, on the west side of Texada Island, when a long way off we saw a large fish boat heading north. We were the "stand on" vessel, meaning that we had the right of way and it was up to the other boat to change course to avoid us. We kept a careful eye on it and our relative courses, but we remained on a collision course. Surely, we thought, they would give way. But they didn't. Sometimes it is dangerous to make a change of course when you are in the stand on position, as it can result in a conflicting move from the other vessel, making the situation worse. So we held our course. We were heading across their bow and they were closing in on us fast. We called on channel 16, we blew our little foghorn; still no change of course. This, remember, was a commercial vessel supposedly run by a professional and experienced crew, and yet that boat never gave way. At the last moment we changed course and avoided a collision, but it left us sweating and breathless. Apparently it's not just novice boaters who need to take a safe boating course.

Still palpitating from our near encounter with Davey Jones's locker, we anchored in another of our favourite spots, Deep Bay on Jedediah Island. Mindful of our previous experience when attempting to leave and head south in inclement weather, we sat in our cozy cabin while the rain pelted on the roof and the wind sang in the rigging. The weather forecast that day, with a Biblical-sounding warning, prophesied waterspouts. Needless to say I wasn't budging. But eventually we caught a break in the weather and headed over to the resort at Schooner Cove on Vancouver Island. That is a great spot to splurge on moorage and have access to a swimming pool, hot tub, laundry and a really nice pub. We sat and watched the coverage of Hurricane Katrina and counted our blessings, which are legion.

Our last night that year was spent in Pirate's Cove on DeCourcy Island, back where we had started our cruise a couple of weeks before. This time Moby stayed glued to our heels and a whole herd of deer or army of squirrels couldn't have tempted him to take off. He'd learned his lesson! It was time to curl up on the couch with his favourite channel, Animal Planet, and dream the winter away.

In 2006, while I was in England, Tomas took the boat to the Silva Bay Shipyard for a major paint job. $10,000 later . . . . I guess I had always know how much money we saved by Tomas doing all the work on the boat, but that bill summed it all up pretty clearly. Nevertheless, despite several trips back over the course of the summer to correct some faulty work, the boat looked pretty sharp with newly painted topsides, snazzy green stripe, repainted mast and complete redoing of the bottom paint.

As the boat was in Silva Bay being retouched, we began our cruise there, with the Spottiswoode cousins delivering us to the boat. That first day we covered 35 nautical miles, fetching up at False Bay on Lasqueti Island. False Bay is named because, despite looking like a nice safe place to tie up or anchor, it is prone to the fierce "Qualicum winds" that whip up in a jiffy and howl down across Georgia Strait from Vancouver Island straight into False Bay. We had been there once before in 1999, and had had a nasty experience in such a wind. We were tied to the dock in a flat calm, but within a few minutes the boat was pitching and rolling and tugging at her lines. We managed to make a not too ungraceful departure and anchored across the bay in a nook, but we lost a paddle from the dinghy and had not been back since. This time the weather looked set fair and we found a good spot to anchor.

Lasqueti Island has a bit of a reputation as a place where the locals are not too friendly. Rumour has it is that this is because the local economy is based on a crop that is not actually legal – you get my drift. In fact, the place does have a slightly Wild West feel to it, with dirt roads, extremely elderly vehicles (some with no licence plates) kicking up clouds of dust as you walk along the road. The residents sport a splendid array of dreadlocks and tie die. One begins to feel that you have entered a time warp – back to the hippy era. However, everyone we encountered was perfectly polite and friendly, so maybe it's just all part of B.C. folklore.

Rather than doing the very long and boring trek up the west side of Texada Island, we decided to backtrack and head up Baynes Sound to Comox, a place we had never visited by boat. Sandy Island, just north of Denman Island, is definitely worth a stop, with a lovely beach walk round the island. We moved over to Henry Bay, on Denman, for the night and continued into Comox the next day, stopping there briefly before crossing Comox Bar and into Georgia Strait. If you look around you as you come out of Comox, it is hard to imagine that so many boats have foundered taking a short cut over the infamous bar, but there is really only one safe place to cross and many have ignored the navigational markers and taken a "short cut" to disaster.

I always feel that our cruise doesn't really begin until we have arrived at the north end of Georgia Strait and are in Desolation Sound and the Discovery Islands, the name for the group of islands that include Quadra and Cortez. It's just over a hundred nautical miles from Salt Spring to either Lund or Heriot Bay, but it usually takes us 3 or 4 days to travel that distance, more if the weather is bad. You just can't be in a hurry when your top speed is 6 miles per hour.

For years I had been tempting my children with tales of sunny days, gourmet meals and choice camping spots on shore, trying to get them to spend a few days with us. That year my daughter Sara, and her boyfriend Bert, agreed to stop off on their way back from a camping trip at Cape Scott. They finally showed up 6 hours late, after I had called the police to find out if they had been in an accident. Having an overactive imagination, I had had gruesome fantasies of them lying mangled in a ditch, so the relief of their safe arrival cannot be overemphasized. I needed a couple of drinks before I could finally relax and enjoy our delicious dinner sitting around our splendid cockpit table. Bert's entry in the logbook the next day, after a day trip over to Manson's Landing reads as follows:

> "I can attest that the above-mentioned trip proceeded with military like precision, and after a lovely day trip, Sara and Bert were delivered on time to their waiting vehicle."

Do I detect a certain tongue in cheek attitude from my "common" son-in-law, as I like to call him? Obviously, I have a better sense of time, schedules and deadlines than they do. Sara has an almost uncanny ability to miss ferries or arrive late for special events. Her most famous late arrival was when she almost missed our wedding. She was coming from Victoria to Salt Spring and arrived panting at the ferry dock just as the boat pulled away. After desperately telling the person at the dock that her mother would kill her if she was late, the captain was radioed and took pity on her, bringing the boat back to pick her up.

Business must have been good that year because as well as repainting the boat we had bought a new dinghy and outboard motor. This new toy proved to be a lot of fun as we could now plane at about 15 knots, with the dogs' ears flying in the wind from their favourite spot – front paws on the bow tube. Whenever I feel guilty (I inherited my father's "careful" attitude to money) about spending money on any non-essential item, I look around at other boats and see how modest ours is, even with our brand new dinghy and motor. Some fairly unpretentious boats are loaded with expensive toys – rubber dinghies that must have cost more than our whole boat is worth, kayaks strapped to cabin roofs, stern rails bristling with fishing gear, fancy awnings and, of course, all the latest in navigational and electronic gadgets.

As well as now having a GPS that records our position and speed, and a fairly new marine radio, our other useful instrument is a depth sounder. The one we had at that time was new sometime in the 1970s, had a rotating red blip that was impossible to see in bright sunshine, and could be set with a dial to read in fathoms or feet. Except for having to unhook it from its mount inside the cabin, and wedge it on the deck with its own personal sunshade, it worked well enough. Then one day it quit. We happened to be in Heriot Bay where there is a splendid second-hand store just up the hill from the dock. The store has a fine selection of household, fishing and marine gear, and browsing through an old box we came across a depth sounder almost identical to the one that had just stopped working. However, this one was one model up from ours and had an alarm that would bleep if you went under a certain depth – hi-tech indeed. Tomas thought it unlikely that it would be compatible to the transducer fitted on the boat, but we bought it for $15 and took it back to try. It worked! And the strange thing was that the old one, when we tried it before disconnecting it, had started working again. So now we have a "modern" depth sounder, complete with alarm, and a spare should it decide to give up the ghost.

After leaving Heriot Bay, we headed to one of our favourite spots, Octopus Islands Marine Park. The new dinghy gave us the means to zoom across to the head of Waiatt Bay where we had heard there was a trail over to Small Inlet on the other side of Quadra – and there it was, just a few steps up from the beach. A gentle stroll along a well-marked trail through a beautiful forest refreshes the soul and makes us count our many blessings. On every trip there seems to be a point, usually about a week in, when the stresses of work and everyday life seem to fade into the background and we can finally relax and start to really enjoy ourselves.

I must have really started to relax, because I didn't check the current tables the next day as we headed through Hole in the Wall. I just left it to Tomas, who assured me that the "little bit of current" would speed us on our way through the Hole. When we got there, however, the water was a boiling mass of standing waves and mini-whirlpools and I baulked. No way was I taking my precious dogs into the jaws of death! We circled about half a mile offshore until the current died down and then proceeded eastwards through the Hole and out into Calm Channel. This is very aptly named as in all the years we have passed through there I have never, ever seen it with more than a light breeze. It is very strange how one gets these "micro-climates" where either it's always blowing up a gale or usually dead calm. On the mainland side of the channel is the old Indian village of Church House. It is long abandoned and the dock has fallen into dangerous disrepair, but the church was still standing in 2006 – just! In the logbook I drew a picture of the building leaning crazily to one side with the encroaching vegetation clearly showing through the windows. Where pews once stood, blackberries now grew in profusion. The cross on top of the steeple still pointed, somewhat drunkenly, heavenward, but I sensed the church would not survive another winter. I was right. We passed it again in 2007 and the middle part of the steeple had collapsed, with the top part balanced precariously on top of the rubble.

As I observed the derelict church through the binoculars, I marvelled at the dogged determination of the early missionaries. This was very much a case of "if Mohammed won't come to the mountain, the mountain must come to Mohammed". In contrast to those who chose to work in residential schools or churches situated in relatively accessible places, these people parachuted into the most remote spots on the coast to bring "the word of God" to the natives. Oh, how well meaning but misguided they were. Many spent decades living in these isolated spots, put enormous effort into erecting European-style churches, only to have them dissolve back into the bush once the settlements were abandoned.

After stopping in Walsh Cove and Pendrell Sound, both of which are beautiful but neither of which have good dog walks, we proceeded to Roscoe Bay, which has a splendid walk up to Black Lake. The bay has a bar across the entrance that makes it impossible for many boats to enter or leave except on a high tide. Because of our shallow draft we can go where many boats cannot. I love watching the faces of other boaters inside the bay as we approach the entrance. "Idiot Boaters", I know they are thinking, "haven't they read their tide tables?" as we glide easily over the bar and choose a spot to anchor. It really is a beautiful and tranquil spot, totally protected from all directions. I wonder if Captain Vancouver found it when he was exploring the area, and if he had whether he would have been so quick to name the area Desolation Sound. Anywhere less desolate on a beautiful August evening would be hard to find.

As we started our slow journey south, we considered making the trip up Jervis Inlet to Princess Louisa Inlet and Chatterbox Falls, a place we had never visited. This is one of the legendary destinations on the coast, but it is 80 nautical miles there and back with very few places to stop along the way, i.e. to walk the dogs. That year we actually did have plenty of time, but after doing yet another careful analysis of the distance and time required getting there, decided once more to give it a miss. Almost every B.C. boater will have a copy of "The Curve of Time" by M. Wylie Blanchet as part of their boat library, and all I can say is that Capi was made of sterner stuff than I am. She went numerous times to the Inlet in a 25-foot wooden boat with no fewer than 5 children and a dog on board! Her stories are told in a matter of fact way, including encounters with bears and cougars that came close to devouring, at the very least the dog, and in a couple of cases one or two of her children. She didn't worry about the dog not getting a walk for a few hours, so why should I? But I do, so no Princess Louisa for us that year.

By this time Tomas had fulfilled a life-long dream to attain his pilot's licence. You would think that having accomplished all that he had since arriving as a penniless refugee 35 years previously, he would have been happy to rest on his laurels. Spend more time on the boat, for example. I would have been very supportive of that plan. Not him; at the age of 55 he started taking flying lessons and graduated top of the class with his Private Pilot's licence in July 2006. He was so keen that in order to do the ground school, which took place every Wednesday night and wrapped up after the last ferry had left for Salt Spring, he would sleep in his car near the ferry terminal. In the middle of winter.

The acquisition of his pilot's licence means that now when we talk about places like Princess Louisa (that we would love to visit but which for us in our slow boat and the paucity of dog walks along the way are somewhat inaccessible) Tomas offers to fly me there. Apparently the next step after learning to fly it to build one's own plane (currently a work in progress), and his eyes gleam at the prospect of an afternoon trip to Princess Louisa in our own flying machine.

He also tempts me, in exchange for supporting his flying habit, with visions of whisking me from our home in Long Harbour to, say, Pender Harbour for lunch. As it would take us about a week to get to Pender Harbour on the boat, that is indeed a tempting thought.

One day we were anchored in Keefer Bay on Savary Island, and a floatplane swooped in and landed. It motored over to the white sandy beach; the pilot hopped ashore, dragged the plane up a few feet on its floats, and unloaded his passengers. I had a vision of us doing the same one day, but in the meantime we have our sturdy *South Islander* whose engine had, to this point in the story, motored us up and down the coast for over 1000 hours.

Having seen what Tomas has accomplished in terms of building our beautiful boat, I have no doubt that should he live long enough the plane will eventually be finished and take to the air. There is one minor problem – I'm terrified of flying! The plane has been designed with room for the two dogs behind the front seats. So even if I decide to stay home, Roz and Moby have the prospect of delightful day trips up and down the coast to some of their favourite walkie spots. I'm just kidding – the dogs will not be permitted to fly unless I pluck up the courage to go along. If we go down, we all go down together!

Once again, at the end of our cruise, *South Islander* brought us safely back to Long Harbour, with a slight change to our normal routine of spending our last night at Conover Cove. This time we anchored at Ruxton Island, which has a wonderful trail around the island, winding past pretty coves, a wetland area, some interesting cabins and, lest one should have run out of suitable boat reading material, a book exchange.

Our return home that year was a little different. While we were away, our dock had finally been finished and the original floating portion was now firmly affixed to the shore by way of a very splendid ramp and walkway. Unloading the boat was now infinitely simpler as we no longer had to make countless dinghy trips back and forth to the beach. We still have to schlep everything up the trail to the house – that motorized, inclined elevator is still not even on the list of "things to do". In the meantime it was time to batten down the hatches for another dark and rainy West Coast winter.

Chapter Ten

2007: Whales, Whales and Yet More Whales

2007 saw us returning to the north end of Vancouver Island, up the fabled Johnstone Strait, for another try at some whale watching. We could never have imagined how lucky we would be that year in our wildlife encounters. If, as a child, someone had told me that one day I would be on a sailboat that was surrounded on all sides by hundreds of dolphins leaping and playing mere feet from the boat, I never would have believed them.

We were determined not to be deterred by weather, and it must have been a fairly easy trip, because despite taking the inside route as far as possible, there is no mention in the logbook of the 25 miles or so of Johnstone Strait that one must travel before you can duck back into the maze of channels. Those prevailing northwest winds, common in Johnstone Strait in the summer, can be a serious deterrent to a cruise to the top of Vancouver Island. This time, however, it seemed to be an uneventful ride up and we had only been out in the Strait a few minutes when a large pod of Orcas passed by a couple of hundred feet away. There is simply no thrill that can compare to seeing those magnificent creatures in the wild. If that had been the only sighting we had, I would have died happy!

The way north had, once again, seen us traversing the fabled tidal rapids, with a very pleasant stop at Blind Channel Resort. This was one of those times we treated ourselves to a slip at the dock instead of anchoring nearby, and it really was worth it. The resort is very well maintained, and there is a good store with post office and Internet access. In addition, there is a wonderful walk through the forest to an 800-year-old cedar tree, one of the behemoths that managed to escape the fate of most of the first-growth forest on the coast. As we stood at the base of the tree and gazed hundreds of feet up at its crown, we tried to imagine what the forests must have been like before white men came along and spoiled most of them by chopping down everything within easy reach of the water. They thought the supply was infinite, but of course it was not. As we cruise up the coast, it is sobering to look around at the remote and seemingly inaccessible terrain and see just how much of it has now been logged. There are no more easy pickings of enormous trees just a few feet from the water; all those were snapped up decades ago. These days, with modern technology, such as helicopter logging, even almost sheer slopes have been denuded.

After another "shrimpy" stop at Lagoon Cove, we ducked into Potts Lagoon to avoid the increasingly miserable weather. The rain drummed on the cabin roof and we had to deal with one of those annoying leaks that seem to be unfixable. The problem is that after a spell of fine weather, the teak deck dries and shrinks, and then when it starts to rain – bingo – the water finds its way along a circuitous route from the deck to a spot right over our bed. How fortuitous that it is Tomas's side of the bed that is directly under the leak! Strangely, during the winter months while she is tied to the dock, and after months of incessant rain, the boat is dry as a bone inside. Ah well – just one of those lovable foibles of our dear *South Islander*.

Even on a rainy, windy day Potts Lagoon is calm and peaceful. We strung our bedding on lines that wound around the cabin, fired up the cozy stove and snuggled down for a day of reading, eating and movie watching. Of course, there are still the dogs to be walked, and this is not a great spot for that activity. I felt a momentary stab of envy for those boaters unencumbered by canine companions, and then we got ourselves suited up in our foul weather gear to give them a toilet break. There is one small island, and we did eventually discover an old and overgrown logging road leading away through the forest, but the dogs' walks were perfunctory. They didn't seem to mind, however, and were quite happy to curl up and doze the bad-weather day away.

The next day we motored over to Harbledown Island, through Beware Passage, aptly named for the number of rocks in the channel, and located the mysterious "Monks Wall". Apparently built by early settlers (and one can only imagine why they bothered) this wall must have been truly impressive before the homestead was abandoned and the wall began to tumble back into the forest. There is one arch left and a couple of almost intact stretches, which gives one a sense of the toil that must have gone into erecting it – for what? It wouldn't even have kept the wilderness at bay, or the wild animals out. This abandoned homestead is a perfect example of the impossibly optimistic dreams of early settlers. In the late 1800s William Herbert Galley and his wife Mary Anne acquired 160 acres on Harbledown Island and built a trading post. Carefully built walls defined the homestead, and the surviving archway marked the entrance to the trading post. It is rumoured that sometime in the 1800s Chinese Buddhist monks inhabited the island, hence the name "Monks Wall". Although these remote areas were home to a surprising number of settlers, it is still hard to imagine that this trading post could have been a viable business. I don't imagine the Galleys did much in the way of a business plan or market research before embarking on this venture – they were, like many others, smitten with a dream of being self-sufficient and living out their lives in this place of spectacular beauty.

What happened next will likely be on the top ten list of unforgettable experiences that I will reflect on when I'm a doddery old lady recounting tales to my grandchildren. We had motored out into Blackfish Sound and started to fish – hoping that the whales, for which this particular area is famous, had left us a salmon or two – when we noticed the water boiling and heaving a mile or so away. The mass of water quickly approached, and as it came closer we saw that it was, in fact, an enormous school of dolphins. We brought in our fishing gear, slowed to a crawl and suddenly the dolphins were all around us. They were leaping, diving, splashing, swimming back and forth under the keel and, most engaging of all, cruising on their sides near the bow with one eye looking up at the boat. I lay on the foredeck hanging over the side as dolphin after dolphin came up, flipped over and eyeballed me from a distance of about 2 feet. It went on for what seemed like hours, but must have been about 30 minutes. Suddenly they seemed to see something more interesting on the other side of the Sound and moved off. If I live to be a hundred I will never forget that experience.

The very next day, after finally catching a salmon thoughtfully left for us by the resident Orcas, we had yet another wildlife encounter. We spotted the whale-watching boats coming our way with a pod of Orcas preceding them. As directed by the powers that be with regard to whale encounters, we stopped our engine and sat and waited. The pod, in three or four smaller groups, were breaching and whacking their tails on the water – how much better could it get? Apparently even better, as four or five of them passed within feet of our stationary boat. Although I had always wanted this to happen, the reality of it was that we were sitting in a thirty-foot boat, and whales as big, or bigger than us, were mere feet away. I know that there has never been a case of a boat being attacked and that the whales, being extremely intelligent beings, are merely curious. But it was, nonetheless, a slightly alarming experience. Just in case one of the whales had spied the tasty morsel of a curious JRT peering over the side and decided that it looked like a rather odd coloured fish, I stowed the dogs safely below.

I'd thought that I'd seen it all, having crossed off a close encounter with Orcas in the wild from my list of "things to do before I die". However, there was more to come. The next day, after another stopover at Alert Bay, we were attempting to repeat our recent fishing success by casting our line around Pearce and Stubbs Islands. We noticed a large colony of Stellar sea lions – huge in comparison to the seals we usually see – and almost simultaneously a solitary humpback whale going round in circles. We stopped the boat and as we watched, a couple of sea lions swam under the dinghy and popped their heads up right beside the boat. The whale and the sea lions appeared to be feeding together, and we watched them from a respectable distance. This solitary whale must have been engaged in what is called bubble net fishing. Normally it's a group of humpback whales (in this case just one) that swims rapidly in circles around and under a school of fish, blowing air through their blowholes. The bubbles form a visual barrier that serves to confine the school within an ever-tighter area. The whale or whales then suddenly swim upwards and through the bubble net, mouths agape, swallowing hundreds of fish in one gulp. This would explain the apparent stupidity of the fish, which didn't seem to have the sense to take flight. The whale and sea lions stayed more or less in the same spot, at least for the 45 minutes that we stayed to watch.

Replete with enough whale sightings to last a lifetime, we headed back into Johnstone Strait for a final treat. Another pod of Orcas passed close by the boat and this one had a baby swimming close to its mother. We had been treated to some of the most spectacular wildlife experiences in the world, and it hadn't cost us a penny! What made all this so amazing was that on our last visit to the area we had seen little or no sign of any marine mammals. Very unlucky the first time, and very, very lucky the second.

The weather had turned wet, cool and foggy, but it was mercifully calm as we motored back down south, stopping in Kelsey Bay for two nights until the worst of the rain had passed. After our usual visit to our friends on Quadra Island, we moved over to Manson's Landing. We intended to anchor there, but it was quite windy and the bay is not a particularly good anchorage except in calm weather, so we decided to move into Gorge Harbour. Folklore has it that eons ago, as one native tribe paddled through the gorge, another warring tribe threw rocks down on them from the top of the almost sheer rock wall.

Sometimes I try to envisage what the coast was like before Europeans came along and spoiled a lot of it by chopping down the trees, catching all the fish, building houses on all the best waterfront spots, installing fish farms in remote and beautiful inlets . . . the list goes one. Still, despite all this, we live in one of the most beautiful spots on earth, a fact I am reminded of every minute we are out on the water.

Our way home that year took us back down the west side of Texada and into the group of islands just north of Jedediah. This looked like a good place to fish, so Tomas set up all the gear and we started to motor slowly back and forth over the chosen spot. Within a very few minutes we had a bite. Now, Tomas, who is the most courteous, sunny tempered personality one could ever meet, has an alter ego when fishing. He becomes your typical macho male who is determined to land the "big one", come what may. My job, according to this alter ego, is to handle the net and land the fish when he brings it close enough to the boat. As I crouched over the bulwarks, net at the ready, he reeled in not a salmon, but a lingcod. Unfortunately I fumbled the net and the fish got away. Never in the years since I had known him had I seen Tomas so angry. One would think I had smashed his precious new car, or worst still, run the boat aground. I couldn't believe this person was my gentle husband. I retreated below in high dudgeon and told him that he could land his own "bleep bleep" fish. After some abject apologies, which I graciously accepted, we cast the line over again. All I can say is that fish must be the dumbest creatures around, because within five minutes we had hooked the same fish for a second time. I know, I know, you'll be saying, how did we know it was the same fish? All I can say is that I'd looked that fish in the eye just before it gave me the finger and escaped the net the first time, and this was definitely the same fish. His second brush with death didn't end so well for him as I adroitly netted him onto the deck before retiring below with the dogs while Tomas delivered the coup de death.

Not knowing much about lingcod, other than it bore a similar name to the fish I grew up on, wrapped in soggy newspaper and doused with malt vinegar, I was somewhat disappointed that we hadn't caught another salmon. Tomas, however, assured me that lingcod was very good indeed. The problem was that with no oven, and not being the sort of fish, like salmon, that you could just slap on the barbeque, I was at a bit of a loss as to how to cook it. Then I had a brainwave. Thinking about that deep fried English cod gave me the idea. As one of the staples on the boat we always carry a supply of Bisquik. It is useful, not just for pancakes, but for making quick bread in a frying pan with a lid. I mixed up a batter using a cupful or so and water, coated the fish with it, and fried it in a little hot oil. I can only say that it was the most delicious fish I have ever tasted, including the freshly caught salmon we had eaten or any gourmet fish meal I had ever had in a restaurant. It bore a faint resemblance to traditional fish in batter, but was less oily and the flavour of the fish shone through its light and crispy coating.

So our wonderful summer cruise wound down and we meandered south via the Sunshine Coast, across Georgia Strait and into our home waters of the Southern Gulf Islands. This had really been one of the best cruises we had ever had, but now it was time to stow the sails and tuck the boat up for another winter on her dock.

Chapter Eleven

2008: Re-Repairs or Why a Boat is Never Fixed

In August 2008 the Spottiswoode cousins, James, Constance, Natasha and Tatiana, escaped the Los Angeles smog and their fast-paced lifestyle for another scenic B.C vacation. This time Natasha's boyfriend, who is rather mysteriously called Post, and their ever so slightly neurotic dog, Luna, swelled the ranks. Luna is a very cultured dog as she spends most of her life in L.A. sitting on the couch listening to Constance giving violin lessons, interspersed with very intellectual conversations between my brainy cousin James, and the rest of the family. This is a household with no TV, which in a city that seems to exist solely for the production of film and television entertainment seems rather odd. In fact for a while James made his living by predicting how much movies would make at the box office, while taking great pride in telling everyone how he seldom, if ever, goes to see one. It's apparently all based on statistics – he inherited from his uncle, my father, an unfathomable skill with numbers.

Luna was fitted with her own PFD and joined the crew on *South Islander* for a number of day trips. One evening we set sail for Portland Island, and as we slowly motored home at dusk we encountered a solitary Orca just off Russell Island. As the sun sank in a blaze of colour and the full moon rose, we watched the whale swim back and forth for over an hour, and managed to capture some unbelievable shots of the whale's dorsal fin against the backdrop of the full moon lighting a swath across the flat calm sea. The cousins were predictably thrilled – not much wildlife to be found in downtown Beverly Hills!

That year we had trouble with both the head and the cutlass bearing. This just goes to show that no matter how much time one spends on maintenance, or in fact on doing major upgrades such as installing the holding tank three years previously, one can never rest on ones laurels and think you might get a break from breaking something. I had naively thought that I would never again have to think about that holding tank sloshing around under our bed, but one day on a short cruise that included an overnight stop in Bennet Bay on Mayne Island, we awoke to a dreadful stink. As I've said before, Tomas is never daunted by the prospect of rolling up his sleeves and getting stuck in so he set to work to determine the problem. Often it is not just one problem, but a perfect storm of several things that result in one major headache. In this case, the light that tells us when the tank is full had malfunctioned, which resulted in pressure building up and loosening the intake valve. I retreated to the foredeck with a book and a clothespin on my nose while Tomas performed a miracle of marine plumbing and fixed everything.

We proceeded on our way out into Georgia Strait, along Belle Chain Islets, where one can almost always see seals, sea lions and eagles, and into Reef Harbour on Cabbage Island. This place has a very special meaning for us, as that is where Tomas had proposed to me in 1999. We had been back several times, but it is not an especially good anchorage as it is totally exposed to the summertime prevailing winds that blow from the northwest. Sure enough, the wind picked up during the night but because of our shallow draft, we'd been able to manoeuvre close to shore and drop anchor in a more protected spot.

Adjoining Cabbage Island, and almost connected to it at low tide, is Tumbo Island, which became part of the new Gulf Islands National Park in 2003. Tumbo has had a very interesting and varied history, including being used for such diverse activities as fur farming and coal mining. Now it is a beautiful and peaceful spot, with a large wetland area and an easy walk that takes one past some old farm buildings to a beach on the south side of the island with spectacular views of Boundary Pass and the San Juan Islands.

We consulted the current tables and timed our exit from Georgia Strait through Boat Pass into Winter Cove to coincide with slack. This is a great short cut, but requires "local knowledge". I just love that term – it implies a salty old sailor who has spent his life plying the local waters. In fact we had done it several times on Coast Guard Auxiliary boats, and it's easy if you know how. The trick is not to approach it head on, but parallel to the shore, watching for the rocks that lie off the Samuel Island point. At maximum current the water roars through the gap, either filling Georgia Strait on a flood or emptying it into Winter Cove on an ebb. I imagine Georgia Strait as a giant bathtub that either has the taps turned on full, or the plug pulled out to drain.

We had arrived in Winter Cove on Saturna Island on July 1st, which is the day of the famous annual Lamb Barbeque. It is almost impossible to find a place to anchor as the harbour is crammed with hundreds of boats, all vying for a spot with room to swing. Once again, our shallow draft came in handy and we were able to wriggle in close to shore and drop anchor.

Seeing how the lambs are barbequed is not for the faint of heart, and especially not for any vegetarians who might be reading this. It is done "Argentinean" style. The lambs are opened flat and skewered whole onto metal crosses that are set into the ground around a huge fire. "Crucified" is the uncomfortable word that springs to mind. The fire is completely circled with the lambs, enough to feed the hundreds who come from far and wide for this community fundraising event. In addition, there is a country-style fair with second-hand stalls, cheap eats and games. We had to take it in turns to visit the fair, as dogs are not allowed. However, there is a short scenic walk that loops from the dock area to Boat Pass, along the Georgia Strait shoreline and back to the dock through the forest.

A year had passed since the Robertson II had run aground on a reef just outside Winter Cove. This historic vessel had been one of the training ships for the Sail and Life Training Society (SALTS), but had recently passed into private ownership. We took the dinghy over to have a look, and what a sad look it was. Only one winter had seen it almost completely stripped down to the bare hull, which at high tide just juts out above the water. How anyone with sufficient maritime experience to be in charge of a 130-foot sailing schooner could have been unaware of the reef is a total mystery. It is clearly marked on the chart, even though it is almost invisible at high tide. It was when attempting to enter the cove in the middle of the night on a high tide that they ran the ship aground, and as the tide fell she became firmly impaled on the rocks. Local salvagers tried everything to get her off, but eventually gave up, and there she remains. The wreck is a visible reminder to all boaters who pass by that reading and understanding their charts is essential.

That year we were severely rationed in the time we were able to take for our summer cruise, due in part to the economic situation which meant that Tomas needed to stay home and work his proverbial butt off in his real estate business, and in part to the fact that we had taken a long vacation in February when we toured Australia in a camper van. That had been our first experience of a RV holiday, and we loved it. We felt as if we were cruising on land, particularly as our campervan was, like *South Islander*, decidedly lo-tech as compared with some of the enormous motor homes we encountered on our travels. As well, the vast distances we covered were reminiscent of the long stretches we spend on the boat getting up to Desolation Sound. 1000 kms at 100 km/h = 10 hours; 100 kms at 10 km/h = 10 hours!

Only having two weeks, instead of the usual three to four, we decided to go as far as the Sunshine Coast, and not try and rush up to Desolation Sound only to have to turn around and head home pretty much as soon as we got there.

The cutlass bearing started acting up again as we were pulling into the anchorage at Newcastle Island, just across the harbour from Nanaimo. It had been a dismal couple of days weather wise, and it now started to pour in earnest. The last thing we needed was an engine problem and as is usually the case, these things happen at the most inconvenient time, this time in the middle of a torrential downpour.

As we had neared the shore, the engine began to make a worrying clunking sound. Once again, Tomas, the wonder mechanic, diagnosed the problem in about 5 seconds flat. Or at least he made an educated guess that proved to be 100% accurate. The cutlass bearing (replaced in Pender Harbour in 2003) had slipped out of its housing, which meant if we continued to run the engine it could destroy the propeller shaft. It had to be fixed before we could continue our cruise. We decided to put the boat up on the beach. Luckily for us Newcastle Island has a perfect beach for our purpose. After carefully checking the chart and the tide tables, and estimating what time the boat would ground and subsequently be exposed, we used the dinghy to tow the boat into shallow, shelving Mark Bay. Anchored fore and aft, she would settle onto the bottom as the tide dropped.

We awoke the next morning with the boat listing to one side, having inadvertently positioned one of the keels over a rock. It's not an exact science, but still works amazingly well. Tomas hopped overboard into the mud and fixed the bearing, although the log notes that "3/4 inch sticking out – may need replacing next year". Better take note of that: it's now 2010 and we didn't replace it last year. That's the thing about making "to do" lists – one does actually have to look at them once in a while!

A word here about Nanaimo. I had always thought of it in terms of its "most malls per capita" reputation with its endless stretches of tract housing interspersed with strip and mega malls, rather than as any sort of interesting destination. It is strategically placed as one leaves the southern Gulf Islands through Dodd Narrows, before making the big leap up the Strait and into Desolation Sound. Because of its location, it is a useful stop for boat fuel and groceries with one of the much maligned malls just steps from the Port of Nanaimo harbour. What we had not realized, until we approached the city from the water rather than the highway, is that the waterfront and downtown area have been seriously revitalized over the past few years. There is a pleasant walk along the waterfront past boutiques and cafes to a nicely landscaped park area. If you walk up the hill a couple of blocks you come to the downtown area. A few years ago it was all but dead, with everyone bypassing it for Mall Land a few kilometres up the highway. Now it is a pleasant district with bookshops, cafes and restaurants as well as the public library where one can access free wifi Internet. The harbour itself has excellent showers and laundry facilities, and moorage is free for a few hours to enable boaters to spend their dollars in the town. It is all neat, clean and well organized with friendly and helpful staff.

Newcastle Island, just across the harbour, is another of our favourite spots. Like many places on the coast it has a very interesting history, with the island's fortunes rising and falling as it went through various incarnations. These included a fish-salting operation, a sandstone quarry and a shipyard. Its sandstone columns were transported across North America to be used in various grand buildings, including the United States Mint in San Francisco. The sandstone was also used to make pulp-stones for grinding pulp into fibre for papermaking. You can still see the remains of the quarry, with some of the machinery still in place, as well as the reverse shapes of the stones left behind in the rock from which the pulp-stones were cut.

In 1931 the Canadian Pacific Steamship Company purchased the island and operated it as a pleasure resort, building a dance pavilion, a teahouse, picnic areas, change houses, a soccer field and a wading pool. The island became very popular for company picnics and Sunday outings, with ships from Vancouver bringing as many as 1,500 people at a time. The pavilion remains standing, a reminder of a different era, but the real charm of the island is its network of easy walking trails. Also, the famous Dinghy Dock Pub on Protection Island is a short trip from Newcastle Island, and a great excuse for a night out with other like-minded mariners.

Getting from south to north, up Georgia Strait, always seems a bit like climbing a very steep hill. Coming home, the trip seems all too fast and we are home before we know it at the end of our cruise. One of the reasons, as I have mentioned before, is the prevailing summertime northwesterly winds. The stretch between Nanaimo, if one travels up the Vancouver Island shore, is long and has few good anchorages. French Creek is a useful stop, about half way between Nanaimo and Denman and Hornby Islands. On our way north that year we stopped in French Creek and made use of their showers, store, pub and, best of all, an excellent fish store with locally caught seafood.

Next day we decided to dash across the Strait to Lasqueti Island before the forecasted gale and we holed up in Scottie Bay for the next couple of days when the gale arrived right on time. This is an excellent protected anchorage, but there is not a lot of room and access ashore is a bit dodgy. We found a place to beach the dinghy at the end of a grassy lane, and discovered a very pleasant walk across the island to False Bay. Along the way one passes everything Lasqueti has to offer in the way of amenities, including a "free" store – the ultimate in recycling – and a very good farm stand with a splendid supply of fresh veggies to go along with our French Creek fish dinner. Unfortunately the bakery was closed for no particular reason. We have yet to taste its wares as it had also been closed on our previous visit. Perhaps one has to arrange in advance for a private viewing of the goods for sale – or more likely it's a well-kept Lasqueti secret. Perhaps it is open only between 10 and 2 on alternate Tuesdays if the moon is in the third quarter and the tide is high.

Hoping for another lingcod – maybe an extended family member of last year's catch – we again fished just north of Jedediah before heading into Deep Bay, one of our favourite anchorages. This time, however, we only caught a spectacularly ugly rockfish. We marinated it and had it for dinner, but it felt a bit as if we were on some kind of "Survivor" challenge, and I wouldn't recommend it unless you are seriously low on provisions.

After a couple of days enjoying the beautiful walks and peaceful anchorage at Jedediah, we decided to cross over to Pender Harbour around the south end of Texada Island. The forecast was for light winds, but this time they got it wrong, way wrong, and before we knew it we were in a very nasty situation. The wind was now blowing hard from the southeast, meaning that the rocky southern end of Texada, which we had to traverse, was a lee shore. The waves were eight to ten feet high, short and steep. The dogs hated every minute of it. We had been butting straight into the wind as we came out of Sabine Channel, so had been motoring. But once we headed east to round the tip of the island we should have raised the sails, which might at least have steadied the boat somewhat. However, when the boat is pitching and rolling alarmingly, I am reluctant to let Tomas out of the safety of the cockpit and up on the cabin roof to deal with the halyards, so we just grit our teeth and motored on. It was dreadful – the exact opposite end of the boating spectrum from my ideal of lounging on the foredeck with a good book and a gin and tonic. If the motor had failed we would have been blown onto the rocks in a jiffy, and the rocks were a seething mass of crashing breakers that looked much too close for comfort.

Once we had passed the end of the island and were able to turn slightly north, we had the wind on our quarter instead of our beam and things got much quieter. When we finally reached the peace and calm of the dock at Madeira Park in Pender Harbour, the boat moored in front of us had a tale to tell. They had done the exact same trip just hours before we had, and their motor had indeed failed. They couldn't get the sail up because the halyard had jammed and they were in serious danger of wrecking their boat. Luckily, a passing boater heard their distress call and towed them into Pender Harbour. The wife was vowing never to set sail again, and I can hardly blame her. One would think that the protected waters between Vancouver Island and the mainland in the middle of summer would be as safe a place to go boating as one could imagine, but it just goes to show that one can encounter adverse weather conditions at any time and in any place.

In fact if you monitor Channel 16 as we do, you would be amazed at the number of boaters who get into trouble. The bottom line is that there is no electronic gadget that can substitute for good old-fashioned knowledge and preparation before casting off the mooring lines and setting sail. It seems hard to believe, but I know of at least two occasions when the boater in distress left port without a chart; one had a forestry map, and the other a paper place mat picked up in a restaurant with a sketch of the local coast. They were both hopelessly lost, and our coastline is littered with rocks and reefs just waiting to jump up and bite those who don't take care. Fortunately both those incidents ended well, but many don't and each year there are several boating fatalities.

Our abbreviated trip ended with another crossing of the Strait from Smuggler's Cove to Silva Bay, and a sunny cruise back to Salt Spring via DeCourcy and Wallace Islands. Much, much too soon our summer cruise was over. We vowed to do better in 2009 and make it back to our favourite cruising grounds, Desolation Sound and the Discovery Islands.

Chapter Twelve

2009: The Border—To Cross, or not to Cross

2009 was one of the hottest summers on record, after a very cold, wet spring. Perfect weather for boating, and boat we did. Our parade of visitors that year began with my daughter, Sara's, in-laws, who came from Ontario for a visit. We took them to Winter Cove and through Boat Pass for the obligatory visitor sightseeing along Belle Chain Islets. Sometimes guests, seeing the B.C. coast in all its splendid summer glory for the first time, make us take a fresh look. We become slightly blasé about the wildlife we see almost every time we go out on the boat, and here were our guests rhapsodizing over seals, sea lions, otters and eagles – wow, how amazing to have these creatures right in our back yard! I'd forgotten that I was brought up in a place where the most exotic wild creatures were rabbits and the occasional fox.

Then, once again, came the Spottiswoode cousins from Los Angeles. This was a very important visit as they officially "landed" in Canada as immigrants. They had fallen in love with Salt Spring on their first visit, bought a house on their second visit, and were now planning to leave LA and move to Canada. Tatiana signed the logbook:

"thanks Captain Tomas and Admiral Mandy".

Now there's someone who knows what's what!

I mentioned in a previous chapter how much harder it had been to cross the border into the U.S. since 9/11, but now's the time to confess that that world-shattering event is not the only reason for our border-crossing difficulties. Way back in the last 1960s, just after arriving in Canada as a refugee, Tomas had a little brush with the law. In fact not having the ability to pay the fine, as well as getting some poor legal advice, he was sentenced to 7 days in Oakalla Correctional Centre for possessing a small amount of marijuana. Subsequently he acquired a pardon, has no criminal record and has been a businessman and outstanding member of our community for decades. At first he had no problem crossing the border and did so many times, but one day in the mid 1980s he and the Diva were flying to Chicago to visit her family and he was refused entry. It seems that his "criminal past", while of no interest to the Canadian authorities, had somehow become a matter of national security to the Americans. Eventually, after writing endless letters and supplying a mountain of documents, he was issued a certificate stating that he was eligible to enter the U.S. This document clearly stated that there was no expiry date; it was good until the day he died. Along with the certificate came a wallet-sized laminated card.

After that he experienced no further problems crossing the border. But after 9/11 things started to change, and not for the better. Every time we crossed, we encountered another level of bureaucracy. One day events really came to a head. Shortly after accidentally dropping his wallet containing the laminated card overboard, but still in possession of the precious piece of paper, we attempted to cross the border.

We were on our way to Idaho to pick up the kit plane that Tomas had ordered. We were towing a custom-built trailer and had a certified cheque for $18,000 safely tucked away. The dream of flying up and down the coast, visiting all those wonderful spots we had previously been to on the boat was about to become a reality. At least it would – three, or four, or maybe five years down the road when he had assembled the 10,000 pieces that comprised the kit!

As we pulled into the border crossing at the Peace Arch we were, as expected, pulled aside and sent inside for a "secondary inspection". But things started to unravel when the border agent told Tomas that his piece of paper was no longer valid. The document stated that it was valid <u>with</u> the laminated card, which he had lost. However, and here's the insanity of the situation, when Tomas had lost that card he had called the appropriate authorities who told him that they no longer issued that particular card. The card would, in fact, have been invalid, and his letter was perfectly valid without it. So even had he still had the card, it would have been null and void, but because he didn't have it they seized on that fact and denied us entry into the U.S. Not being the sort of people who take this kind of mad bureaucracy lying down we began to argue – not a good move when the people you are arguing with are toting a personal arsenal. We pointed out that Tomas had been crossing the border for the last 20 years with a document issued by their State Department, that the offence had not even taken place in the U.S., that in any case he had no criminal record in either country, that he was an upstanding citizen, and finally, and I think most to the point, that we were entering the country to boost their economy by purchasing a big-ticket item, i.e. an airplane.

At some point in this lengthy wait, I had needed to use the bathroom. I was told by a large, bullet-headed man with a buzz cut, that "Ma'am, we don't have a bathroom here – you'll have to go back to Canada to use theirs." I'm not kidding, that's what he said! I burst into tears, and a female agent who was sympathetic to me and a couple of others who had been waiting for hours, allowed us to use the bathroom. But I'd just about had it, and vowed never to visit this dreadful country again.

Finally that same female agent came up with a solution. She overruled the agent we had been dealing with and asked Tomas if he would mind being "paroled" into the U.S. for a limited-time entry. We sighed with relief and paid the $71 for the entry visa without a murmur.

And that's why we had been so reluctant to attempt crossing the border in our boat. We'd done it in 2005, but felt that maybe we'd just been lucky and shouldn't test our luck too often. However this year we felt brave enough to give it another try, so one sunny day in July we headed over to Roche Harbour, passports and precious paper at the ready.

The rules state that everyone except the Master of the vessel must stay on board until the boat has cleared Customs and Immigration. So I waited below as Tomas bearded the lion in the den – as in the agent in his booth on the dock. I waited, and I waited, and I waited. After about an hour, I was getting desperate and wondered if I'd be thrown in jail for stepping off the boat to enquire about the whereabouts of my husband. Just as I was plucking up courage to go ashore Tomas returned, with a large grin on his face. It seemed that the border agent was as friendly as the one we'd encountered on our last visit, but this guy had gone out of his way to help. Recognizing the absurdity of the situation, he had sent one of his deputies across the island to his office in Friday Harbour to bring him a special stamp. That was why it had taken so long, but the resulting document was a six-month visa for unlimited entries into the U.S.

On the basis of that document we later booked a trip to Costa Rica for January 2010, timed to return through the U.S. before the visa expired. And here's the ultimate irony – when we got to U.S. Customs at Vancouver Airport on our way down to Costa Rica, and despite having a completely valid visa with all the appropriate stamps that did not expire for another month, we were again pulled aside. They did not recognize the visa as being valid, even though it had been issued by one of their own agents, and we were made to jump through the hoops all over again. Suspicious perusal of Tomas's original document, questions about his past, much tapping into the computer with grim looks and shaking of heads. Eventually he was issued another visa valid just long enough to get us back through the U.S. on the way home.

However, back to the summer of 2009. Thrilled with the seemingly valuable visa and heartened by the humanity of this particular official, we spent a couple of hours in Roche Harbour sweltering under a brilliant blue sky with the temperature hovering in the 30s, before pushing off from the dock and anchoring at Turn Island State Park for the night.

There was a large group of teenagers camping on the island, and when we went ashore the campsite, outhouses and picnic area were a mess. This was the first time I'd seen so much as a scrap of litter in any of the State Parks we had visited, so the next day when we stopped at Jones Island State Park, I approached a park ranger and mentioned the poor condition of Turn Island. The poor man went pale, apologized over and over, immediately got on his radio and called out the cavalry. I have no doubt that by the end of the day Turn Island was back to its pristine state.

The weather continued to be blisteringly hot as we wended out way around the islands, fetching up in Blind Bay on Shaw Island. We found a pleasant spot to anchor and took the dinghy to explore the surrounding area. Apart from anything else, travelling at 15 knots gave us a chance to cool off. The dogs perched on the bow tube, ears flying in the wind. The dinghy was "their" boat and it was a great relief after sweltering on the hot teak deck of *South Islander.*

The next morning a strange sound of chirping and tweeting awakened us from our peaceful slumbers. Looking up through the open forehatch we saw a whole flock of swallows lined up on the lifelines. Every so often, one would take of, circle the boat and alight again. More kept joining the throng, and as we lay quietly observing this beautiful sight, one landed on the rim of the forehatch and peered down at us lying below. Others bravely joined in, and soon there were half a dozen heads watching us and cheeping merrily. Of course the inevitable happened; one of the dogs barked at this strange sight and the whole flock took of in one whoosh of wings.

The next day, anchored in Prevost Harbour on Stuart Island, the CBC announced that it had been the hottest day on record in Vancouver – 34 degrees. We motored home via Bedwell Harbour, over flat calm, glassy seas, thanking our lucky stars that we had the boat.

Weather wise, it really was the most amazing summer. Here once again are my totally unscientific weather statistics for our 19-day main cruise:

> 10 days just pure sun and either hot or very hot
> 5 days sunny with a bit of cloud, but still very warm
> 1 cloudy day
> 3 days cloud with a bit of rain

We visited our usual favourite spots, Lund, Savary, Von Donop, Squirrel Cove, Octopus Islands and Tenedos Bay. It seems that although we visit many places over and over again, we often discover something new at one of our familiar stops. That year we discovered a splendid new walk from Waiatt Bay (close to Octopus Islands) to Newton Lake. It is about an hour's walk from the bay, with only one steep part and the prospect of a refreshing swim for all of us at the end. Most of the people we meet on our walks also have dogs, which leads me to believe that many boaters never go ashore. Sure, sometimes when it's pouring with rain, I'd much rather stay toasty in front of the stove with a good book, but we have explored so much more on our coastal travels by the very fact that we have the dogs. They must have added at least ten years to our lives.

Sara and Bert met us at Okeover Inlet for, supposedly, one night on the boat. They ended up spending three days. The trip started out as a duty visit to the parents – I had been begging them for years to join us on the boat for a few days – but after a day of lazing on the foredeck, being fed gourmet meals at regular intervals with the added service of an open bar, they began to see that cruising with parents had definite advantages.

They had just returned from a camping trip to the Brooks Peninsula, so no doubt our proposed mini-cruise seemed a tad tame. However, for the first night we went into Theodosia Inlet. With their pit bull, Elly, sitting amidships, they took their canoe and explored the estuary. It was the most sublime evening and the estuary was quiet and devoid of other human presence. They were gone for hours, and returned to a delicious crab dinner (no, we hadn't caught them; they had been given to us by a very nice man at the Okeover dock) accompanied by an extremely good bottle of wine we had been saving for years, all eaten as dusk fell over this magic place. Money cannot buy an experience like that. Earlier they had scoped out a perfect camp spot up on a mossy bluff, and the three of them paddled ashore to spend the night in a place just as quiet and remote as the Brooks Peninsula. They were impressed enough to agree to another day on the boat. What is it about young people that they never ever make firm plans in advance? And especially where parents are concerned, always leave the option open to depart at a moment's notice.

We wanted to show them some of our other favourite places, so we spent a night in Grace Harbour, and another in Tenedos Bay. Grace Harbour was not as peaceful as it usually is because a large boat ran its generator late into the evening. I cannot understand how people can come into a pristine anchorage and fire up a loud machine just so they can watch their big screen TV and run their microwave. It totally defeats the purpose of getting out into the wilderness. On the plus side, Bert, Sara and Elly had the campsite to themselves.

In Tenedos Bay our suggested camp spot on the bluff overlooking our anchorage was spurned. Bert had consulted his portable GPS and decided that Unwin Lake looked interesting enough to explore by canoe. We helped them schlep the canoe and their camping gear up the trail from the bay to the lake and they paddled off into the sunset. Next day, when they had missed the appointed departure time by several hours, I started to get a bit anxious – as in imagining a full-scale search and rescue mission. I could see the headlines: "Young B.C couple and pit bull terrier missing in wilderness – search continues". Just as I was starting to seriously consider calling the Coast Guard, and after I'd spent hours sitting on a rock gazing out at the lake, they appeared. They'd just lost track of time and their comment was, "we're on holiday, aren't we, what does a couple of hours matter?" Quite right too, I must learn not to be such a clock-watcher!

After dropping Bert and Sara back at Okeover where their vehicle was parked, we started to wend out way home. We stopped at the Copeland Islands overnight and found out later that the kids had canoed over from Lund and were actually camped on the other side of the same island. They were about 100 metres away watching the same, spectacular sunset over Georgia Strait as we were. Obviously you can only take so much of parents, even those with unlimited food and drink on tap.

On the long haul down the Sunshine Coast side of Georgia Strait, we stopped at Sturt Bay on Texada Island. This is a great spot to duck into if the weather gets rough out in Malaspina Strait. One year we stayed there for three days as a strong north westerly howled down the strait. We made friends with others at the dock and even got invited to a local resident's home for dessert one evening. This time we stopped only for lunch and to pick the huge blackberries I knew of from previous visits. As we are usually cruising in late August, one of our favourite desserts is stewed blackberries and apples, since apples are easy to find in the many abandoned orchards up and down the coast.

Smuggler's Cove is one of the most perfect, protected anchorages along this stretch of coast, and there is a wonderful doggie walk along an interpretive trail. The cove is so tucked away and has so many nooks and crannies that it is easy to imagine it as a refuge for the rum-runners. During Prohibition in the 1920s they used the Cove to store bootleg liquor en route from stills on Texada Island to rum-running boats heading to the US.

Once again, our last stop was Conover Cove on Wallace Island, and this time we had an unexpected and charming wildlife encounter. We had tied to the dock and were awakened at 5 a.m. by the pitter-patter of tiny feet on the deck. Then the noise stopped, and we looked up at the main hatch to see two racoons, mother and baby, with their paws on the rim of the hatch, gazing at us from their incredibly cute bespectacled eyes! Of course, one surprised woof from Moby and they took off, running up the ramp and into the bushes.

Over the years I've become so attached to our boat, that I think of her as having a distinct personality. She has been part of so many wonderful experiences, and has taken care of us so well, that I feel she deserves the very best care and attention. As we secured her once more on her dock in Long Harbour I laid my hand on the cabin roof and promised that we would tackle that "to do" list and make 2010 the year that she leaves the dock with no job undone – fresh paint on the roof, new sign on her stern, the tiles behind the stove regrouted, all missing deck plugs replaced and her brightwork touched up, to name just a few! It was going to be a busy spring next year with yet another summer of cruising to look forward to.

Epilogue

I hope that the stories in this book have, even for the most experienced boaters among you, given you a glimpse of places that you now may be inspired to visit. Boating in the waters between Vancouver Island and the mainland of British Columbia must be one of most sublime travel experiences on this planet. Even after many years of visiting the same places over and over, I am always stunned by the beauty and diversity of what I see when I glance up from my preferred spot on the foredeck. If a refugee from a land-locked country and an immigrant from one of the tamest countries in the world can embrace cruising our waters with such enthusiasm, then anyone can. It doesn't even take a relatively comfortable boat such as ours to go cruising. We have seen some really small boats where the passengers camp ashore and even kayaks with a dog perched in the second seat. If you do your homework and take a safe boating course, the cruising areas I have described can be accessed by almost anyone.

Roz is now thirteen years old, and Moby has just had his tenth birthday (suitably celebrated with his sister, half brother and mother, a special dinner and a doggie movie). Apart from being completely deaf and slightly less active, Roz is still keen to jump on and off the boat and take part in all shore excursions. Moby never seems to change other than sporting a few grey hairs and an even keener attachment to the couch.

We, on the other hand, have embraced new interests that sometime threaten to impinge on our boat time. As I have previously mentioned, Tomas is building a plane in the garage, and as I write this is just about ready to cover the tubular steel fuselage. Somewhat alarmingly for me, the plane is not sheeted in metal, but with a special fabric which is then coated with layers of some hi-tech version of the dope they used at the dawn of the aviation age. I'm assured that it is as strong as metal, and I have seen several examples of finished planes, some of which actually fly. But I still remain somewhat trepidatious of taking to the sky in a plane made of tubing and fabric. At least I won't have to worry about it for a while; test flights are not scheduled for another year or two.

I now have a horse named James who takes up a lot of time and whose care is a concern whenever we go cruising. Recently we moved him from a boarding situation to our neighbour's property, at which point we had to buy him a pony to assuage his loneliness. So we became the besotted owners of Princess Pretty Penny, a miniature horse who is so small she can pass under James' belly.

As I write this, in June 2010, the boat has been cleaned top and bottom and is ready to "hit the road", but we have yet to take her out of the harbour. Last winter, while we were away in Costa Rica (remember that U.S. visa?) there was a tremendous storm that threatened to tear her off the dock. Fortunately our neighbour sprang to action and clawed his way out on the heaving dock to replace the lines, but she sustained considerable cosmetic damage that is still not completely fixed. We hope to have her all spruced up and that pesky list of things to do addressed before our summer cruise, but it's a struggle to get everything done. In addition to all of the above, the new dock required a new path up to the house, and that is still a work in progress.

We now talk constantly about "retirement", which will take place who knows when, but hopefully before we're too old to enjoy it. When that much-longed for day arrives, we plan to spend a lot more time on the boat.

In the meantime I can see the boat out of the kitchen window, and yearn for those long, lazy summer days when the only question is when to rouse myself from my hammock and take our next walk ashore, or whether to choose gin and tonic or Pimm's for a pre-dinner drink!

~KEY~

Camping

Outhouse

Safe Anchorage

Water Pump

Marsh

Mooring Buoy

Lighthouse

Orchard

Beach Access

Dock

Trail

Cliffs

Road

Lookout Bench

Bike Trail

Picnic Bench

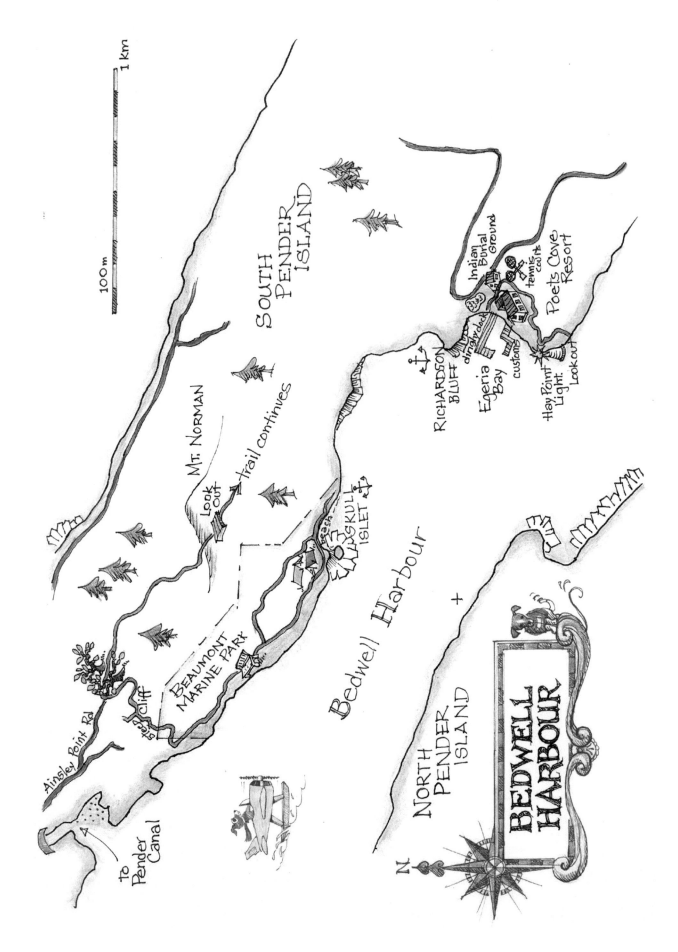

1 km

100 m

SOUTH PENDER ISLAND

Indian Burial Ground

Poets Cove Resort

tennis courts

dinghy dock

RICHARDSON BLUFF

customs

Egeria Bay

Hay Point Light

Look out

MT. NORMAN

Look Out

trail continues

SKULL ISLET

beacon

Bedwell Harbour

Beaumont Marine Park

Steep cliff

Ainsley Point Rd

to Pender Canal

NORTH PENDER ISLAND

N

BEDWELL HARBOUR

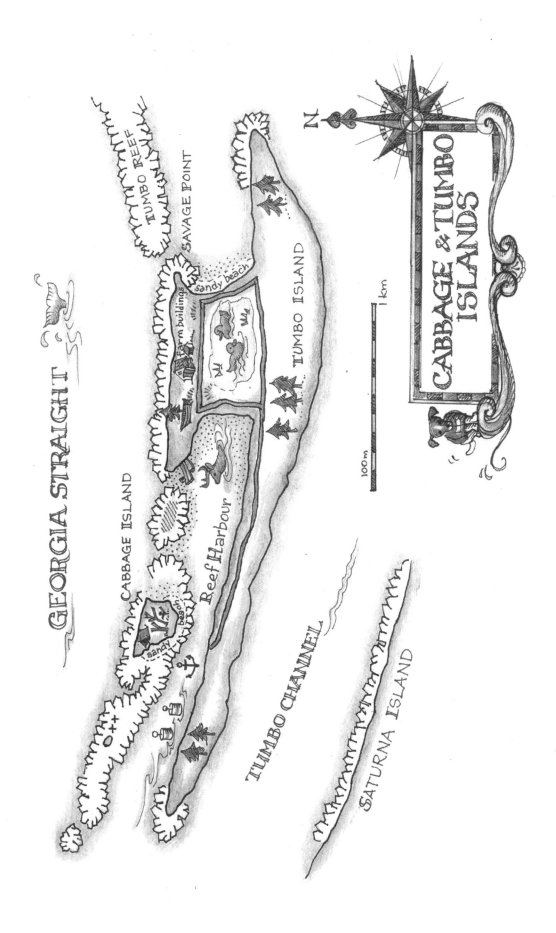

GEORGIA STRAIGHT

TUMBO REEF

SAVAGE POINT

sandy beach

Farm buildings

CABBAGE ISLAND

sandy beach

TUMBO ISLAND

Reef Harbour

TUMBO CHANNEL

SATURNA ISLAND

CABBAGE & TUMBO ISLANDS

N

1 km

100 m

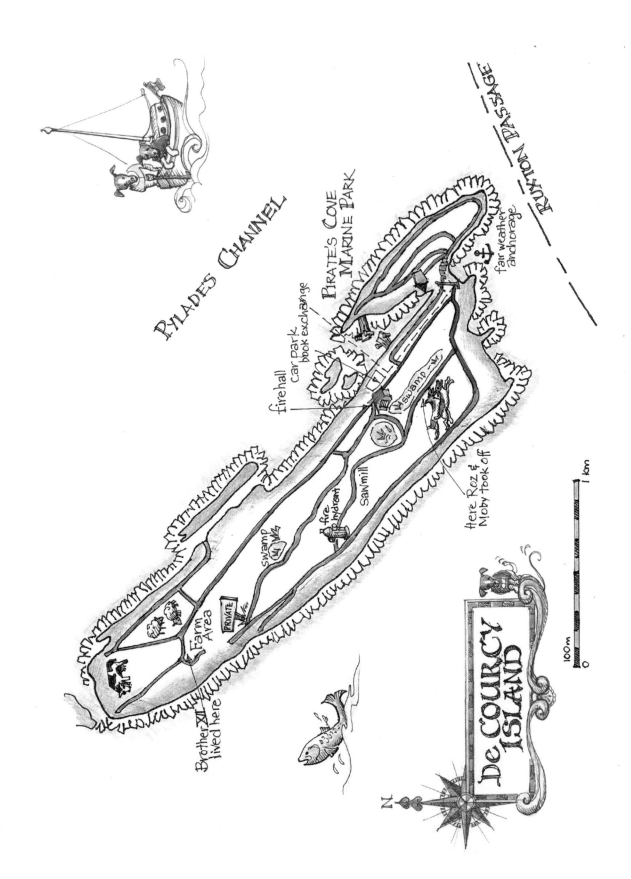

PYLADES CHANNEL

RUXTON PASSAGE

PIRATE'S COVE
MARINE PARK

fair weather
anchorage

firehall

car park
book exchange

swamp

swamp

fire
hydrant

sawmill

Here Roz &
Moby took off

PRIVATE

Farm
Area

Brother XII
lived here

De COURCY
ISLAND

N

100m   1 km

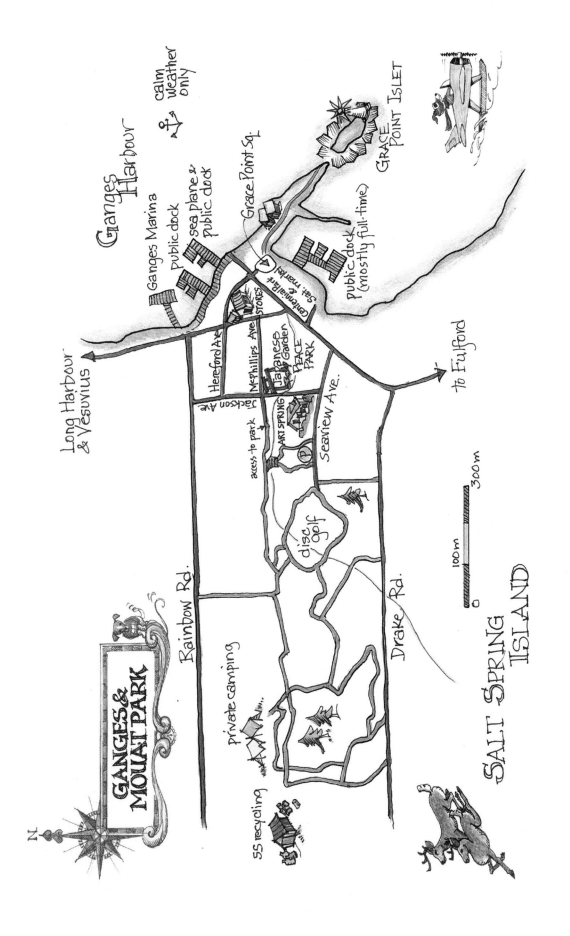

Ganges Harbour

calm weather only

Ganges Marina
Public dock

sea plane &
public dock

Grace Point Sq.

Grace Point Islet

public dock
(mostly full-time)

Long Harbour
& Vesuvius

STORES

Centennial Park
Sat. market

Hereford Ave.

McPhillips Ave.

Jackson Ave.

Japanese Garden

PEACE PARK

ART SPRING

access to park

Seaview Ave.

To Fulford

disc golf

Rainbow Rd.

Drake Rd.

private camping

SS recycling

100m   300m
0

N

GANGES &
MOUAT PARK

SALT SPRING ISLAND

N

GRACE
HARBOUR

GIFFORD
PENINSULA

swimming
off rocks

old
logging
equipment

camping

dinghy
landing

Grace
Harbour

to Isabel
Bay

trailhead
flagged

Isabel Bay

Jean
Island

Malaspina Inlet

Scott
Point

Moss
Point

Salubrious
Bay

Edith
Island

Malaspina
Peninsula

Selina
Point

100 m

1 km

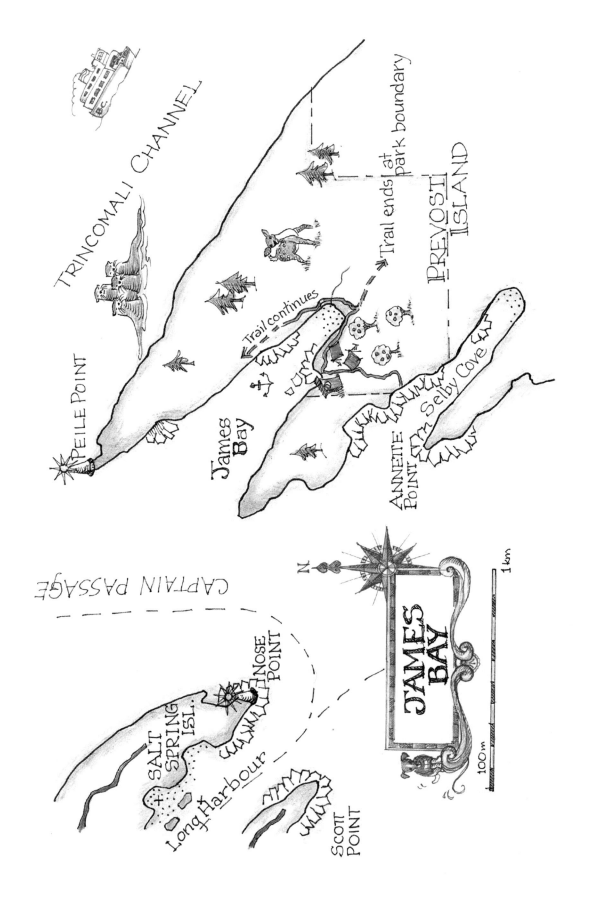

TRINCOMALI CHANNEL

B.C.

PEILE POINT

Trail continues

Trail ends at park boundary

PREVOST ISLAND

James Bay

Selby Cove

ANNETTE POINT

CAPTAIN PASSAGE

NOSE POINT

SALT SPRING ISL.

Long Harbour

SCOTT POINT

N

JAMES BAY

100 m

1 km

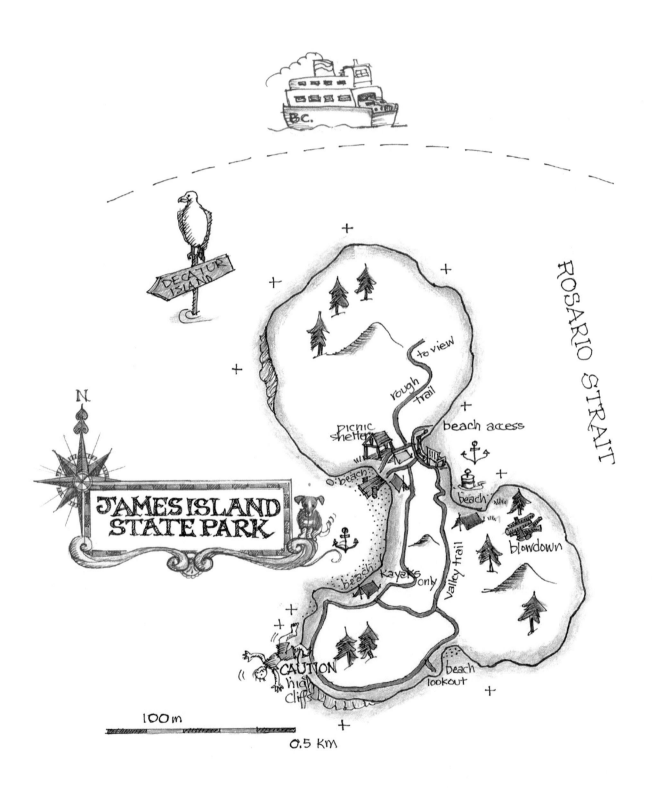

ROSARIO STRAIT

DECATUR ISLAND

B.C.

N

JAMES ISLAND
STATE PARK

to view

rough trail

picnic shelter

beach access

beach

beach

blowdown

Valley trail

Kayaks only

beach

CAUTION high cliffs

beach lookout

100 m

0.5 Km

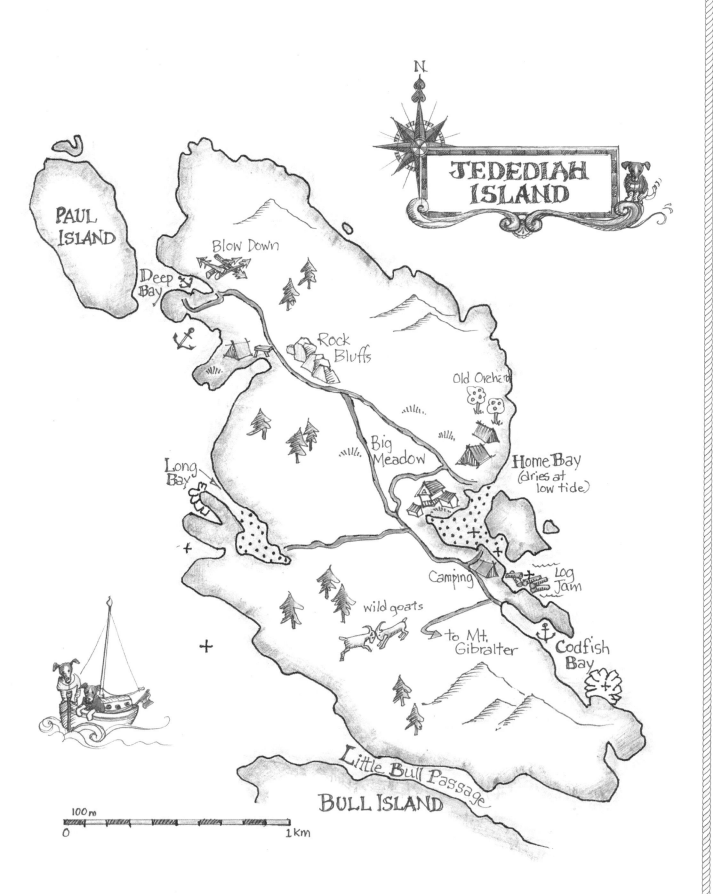

PAUL ISLAND

JEDEDIAH ISLAND

N

Blow Down

Deep Bay

Rock Bluffs

Old Orchard

Big Meadow

Home Bay
(dries at low tide)

Long Bay

Camping

Log Jam

wild goats

to Mt. Gibralter

Codfish Bay

Little Bull Passage

BULL ISLAND

100 m

0   1 km

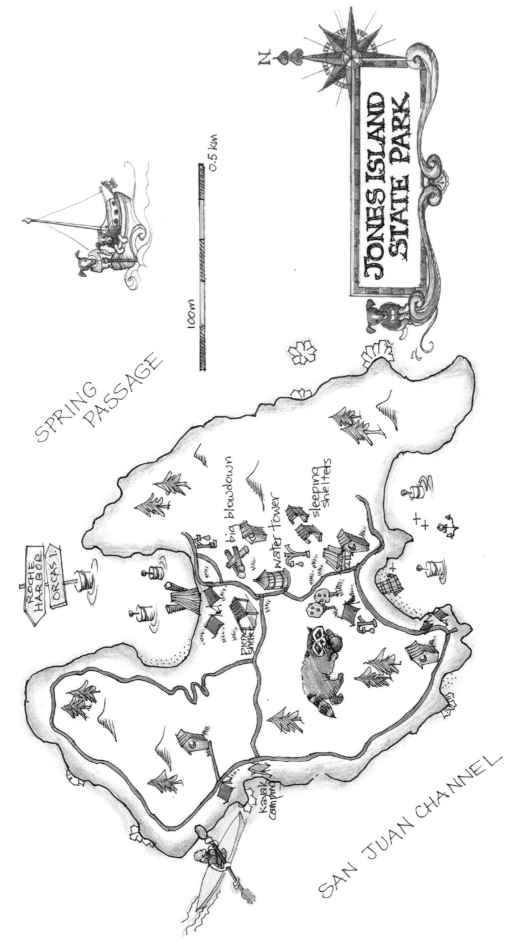

JONES ISLAND STATE PARK

N

0.5 km

100m

SPRING PASSAGE

ROCHE HARBOR
ORCAS I.

big blowdown

water tower

sleeping shelters

Picnic
shelter

Kayak
camping

SAN JUAN CHANNEL

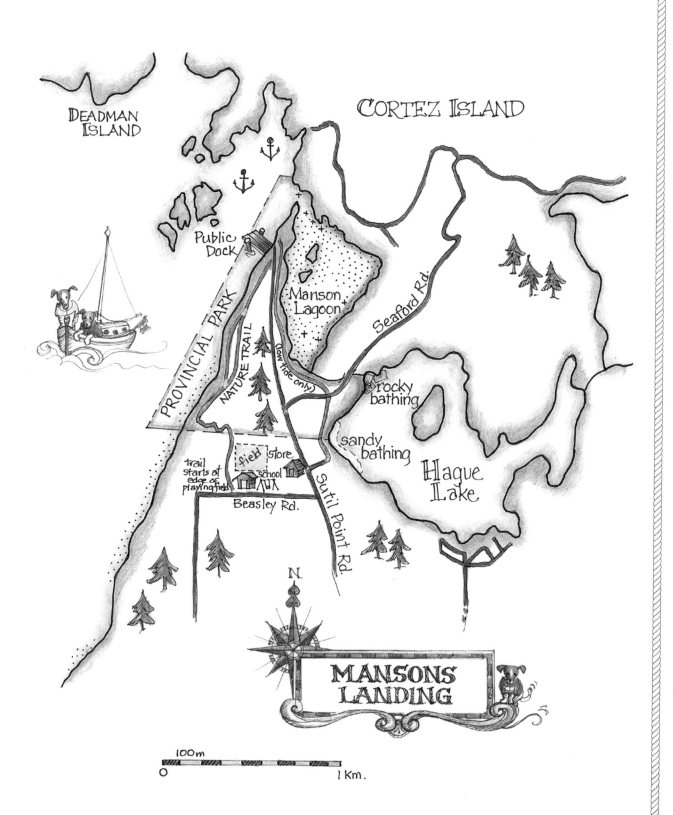

DEADMAN ISLAND

CORTEZ ISLAND

Public Dock

PROVINCIAL PARK

NATURE TRAIL

Manson Lagoon

(low tide only)

Seaford Rd.

rocky bathing

sandy bathing

Haque Lake

trail starts at edge of playing field

field

store

school

Beasley Rd.

Sutil Point Rd.

N

MANSONS LANDING

100 m

0   1 Km.

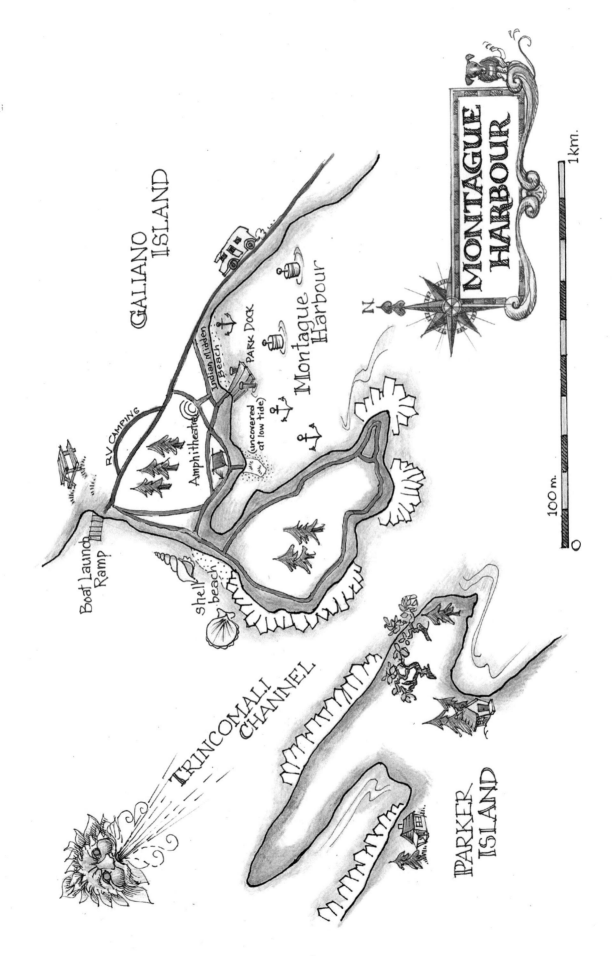

GALIANO ISLAND

RV CAMPING

Boat Launch Ramp

Amphitheatre

Indian Midden

Beach

Park Dock

(uncovered at low tide)

shell beach

Montague Harbour

MONTAGUE HARBOUR

N

1 km.

100 m.

0

TRINCOMALI CHANNEL

PARKER ISLAND

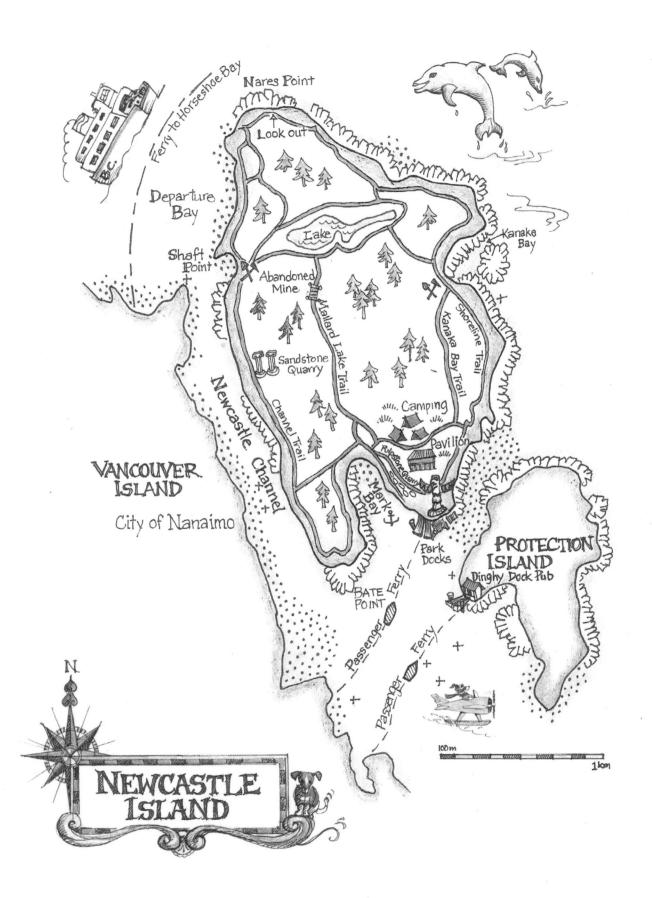

Ferry to Horseshoe Bay

B.C.

Nares Point

Look out

Departure Bay

Shaft Point

Abandoned Mine

Lake

Kanaka Bay

Shoreline Trail

Kanaka Bay Trail

Mallard Lake Trail

Sandstone Quarry

Channel Trail

Newcastle Channel

VANCOUVER ISLAND

City of Nanaimo

Camping

Pavilion

Pulpstone Quarry

Mark Bay

Park Docks

BATE POINT

Passenger Ferry

Passenger Ferry

PROTECTION ISLAND

Dinghy Dock Pub

N

NEWCASTLE ISLAND

100 m

1 km

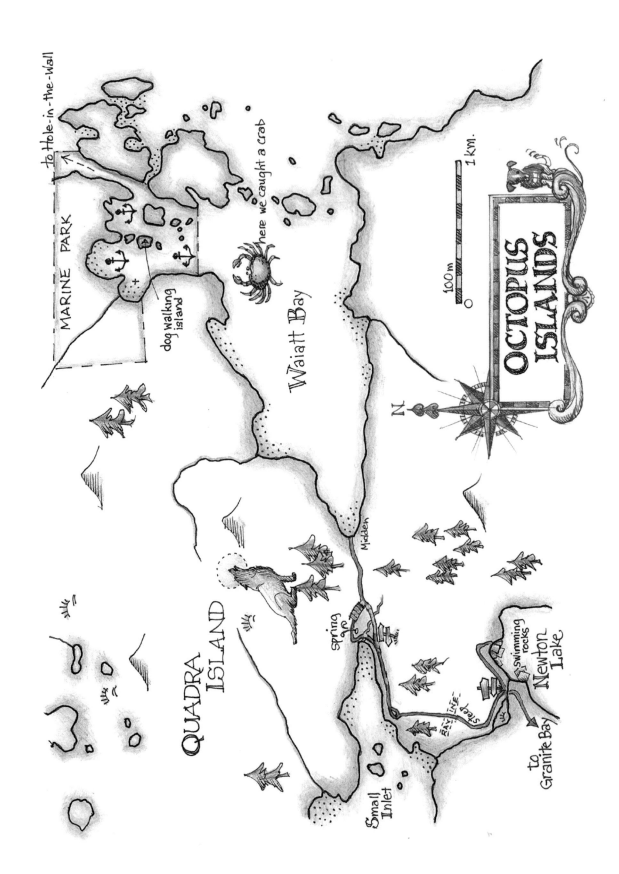

to Hole-in-the-wall

MARINE PARK

dog walking island

where we caught a crab

Waiatt Bay

QUADRA ISLAND

Small Inlet

Midden

spring

RAVINE-site-

Swimming rocks

Newton Lake

to Granite Bay

OCTOPUS ISLANDS

N

100 m   1 km.

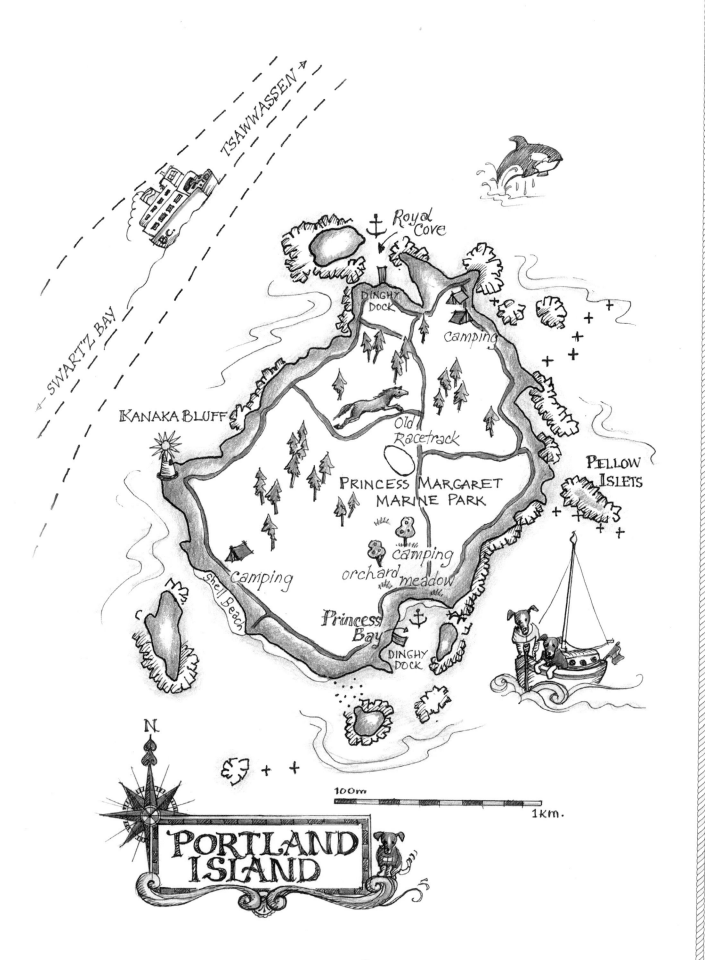

TSAWWASSEN →

SWARTZ BAY →

B.C.

Royal
Cove

DINGHY
DOCK

camping

KANAKA BLUFF

Old
Racetrack

PRINCESS MARGARET
MARINE PARK

PELLOW
ISLETS

camping
orchard meadow

camping

Shell Beach

Princess
Bay

DINGHY
DOCK

N

100m
1km.

PORTLAND
ISLAND

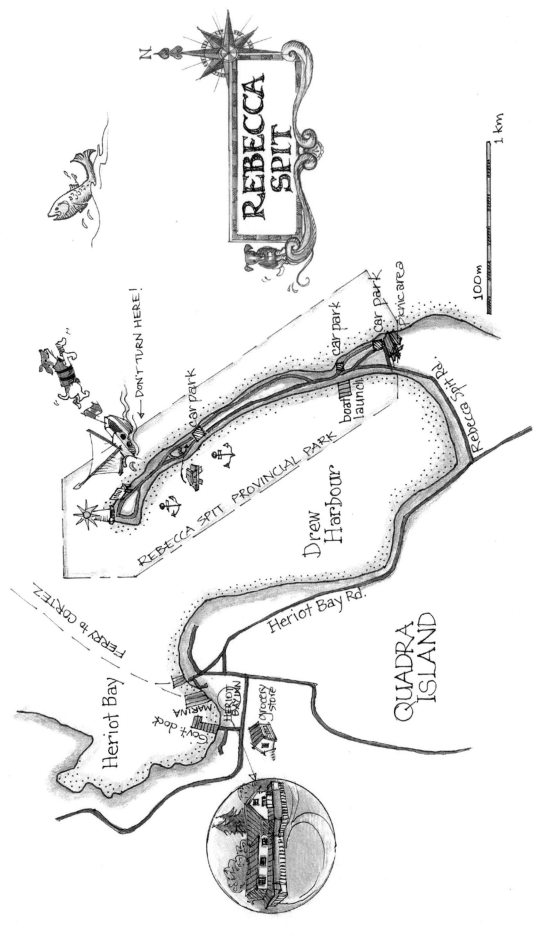

REBECCA SPIT

N

1 km
100m

DON'T TURN HERE!

car park

car park

car park

Picnic area

boat launch

REBECCA SPIT PROVINCIAL PARK

Rebecca Spit Rd.

Drew Harbour

FERRY to CORTEZ

Heriot Bay Rd.

Heriot Bay

Gov't dock

MARINA

HERIOT BAY INN

Grocery Store

QUADRA ISLAND

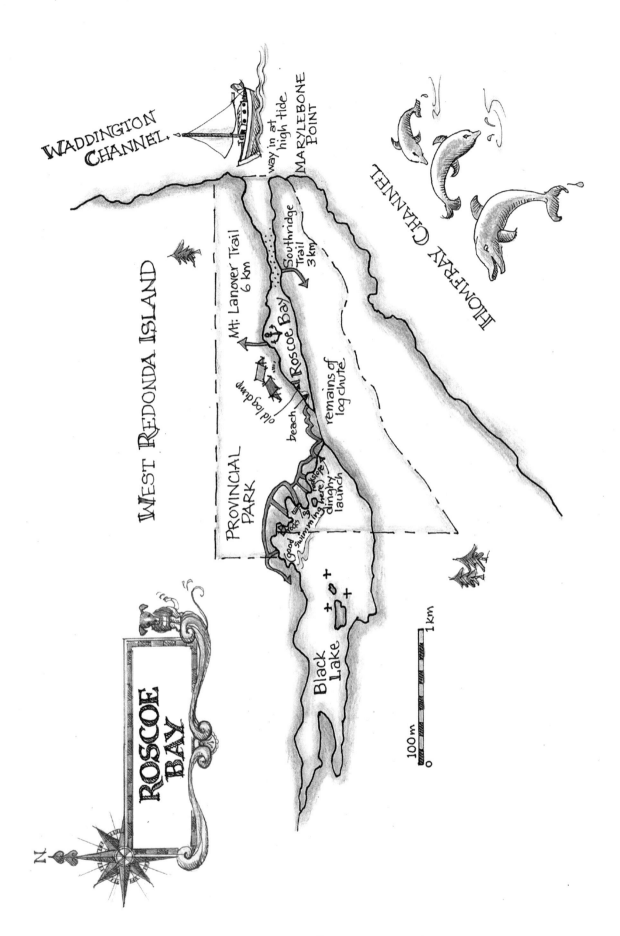

WADDINGTON CHANNEL

way in at high tide

MARYLEBONE POINT

WEST REDONDA ISLAND

Mt. Lanover Trail 6 km

Southridge Trail 3 km

Roscoe Bay

old log dump

beach

remains of log chute

PROVINCIAL PARK

Good rocks for swimming here

dinghy launch

Black Lake

HOMFRAY CHANNEL

ROSCOE BAY

N

100 m

1 km

0

— 87 —

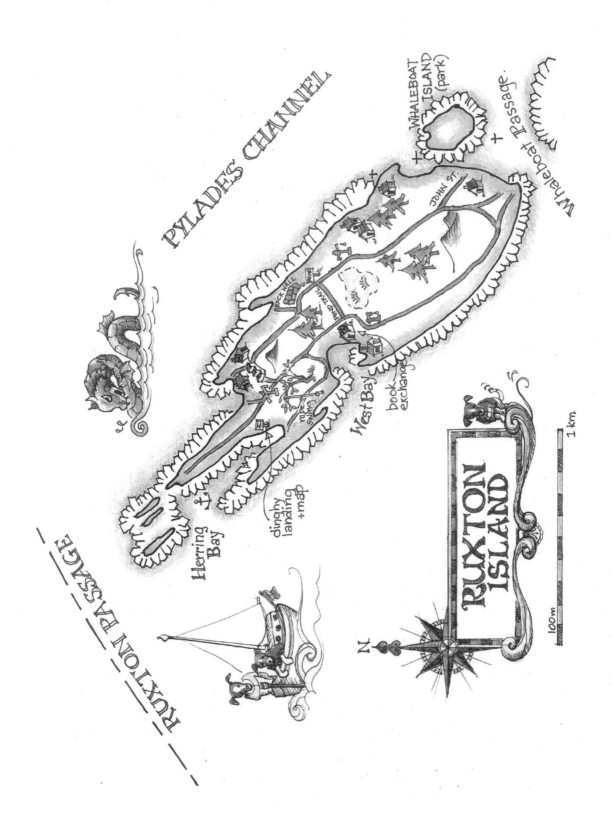

PYLADES CHANNEL

RUXTON PASSAGE

WHALEBOAT ISLAND (park)

Whaleboat Passage.

JOHN ST.

ROCK HALL

West Bay

book exchange

Herring Bay

dinghy landing +map

RUXTON ISLAND

N

100m   1 km

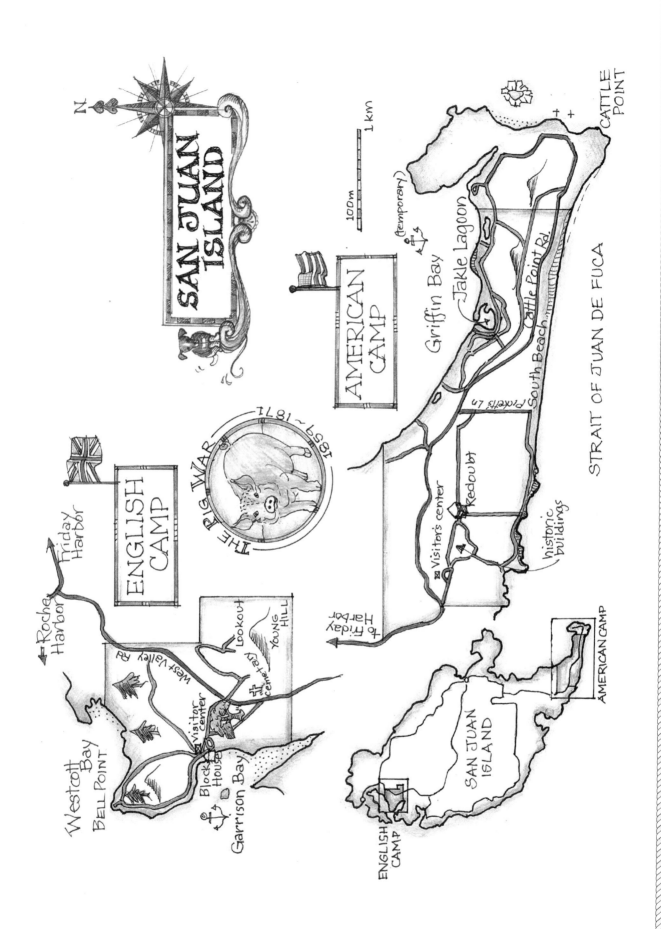

SAN JUAN ISLAND

N

THE PIG WAR 1859 ~ 1871

ENGLISH CAMP

← Roche Harbor
Friday Harbor →

Westcott Bay
Bell Point
West Valley Rd
Lookout
Cemetery
Young Hill
Visitor Center
Block House
Garrison Bay

AMERICAN CAMP

1 km
100m

Griffin Bay
(temporary)
Jakle Lagoon
Cattle Point Rd.
South Beach
Picketts Ln.
Redoubt
Visitor's center
historic buildings
to Friday Harbor

CATTLE POINT

STRAIT OF JUAN DE FUCA

SAN JUAN ISLAND
ENGLISH CAMP
AMERICAN CAMP

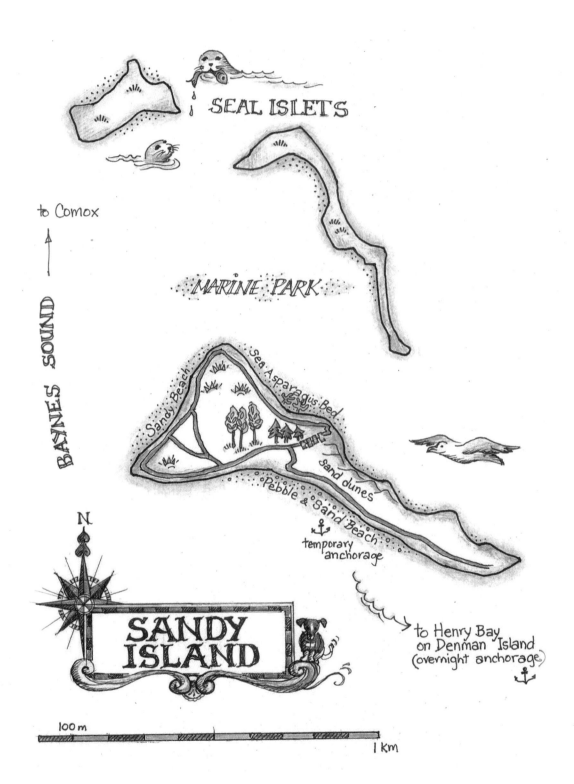

SEAL ISLETS

to Comox

MARINE PARK

BAYNES SOUND

Sandy Beach

Sea Asparagus Bed

sand dunes

Pebble & Sand Beach

temporary anchorage

N

SANDY ISLAND

to Henry Bay on Denman Island (overnight anchorage)

100 m

1 km

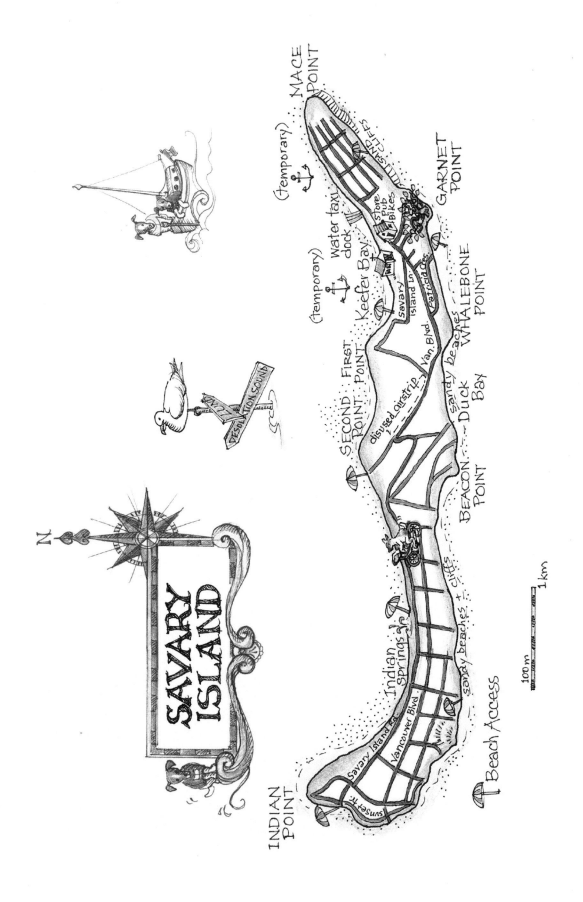

SAVARY ISLAND

N

DESOLATION SOUND

INDIAN POINT

Indian Springs

Savary Island Rd

Vancouver Blvd

sandy beaches + cliffs

sunset tr.

Beach Access

100 m   1 km

Second Point

First Point

disused airstrip

Island Ln

Savary

Van Blvd

Patricia Cres.

sandy beaches

Keefer Bay

(temporary)

(temporary)

Water taxi dock

Store Pub Bikes

GARNET POINT

CRYSTAL CLIFFS

MACE POINT

(temporary)

WHALEBONE POINT

Duck Bay

BEACON POINT

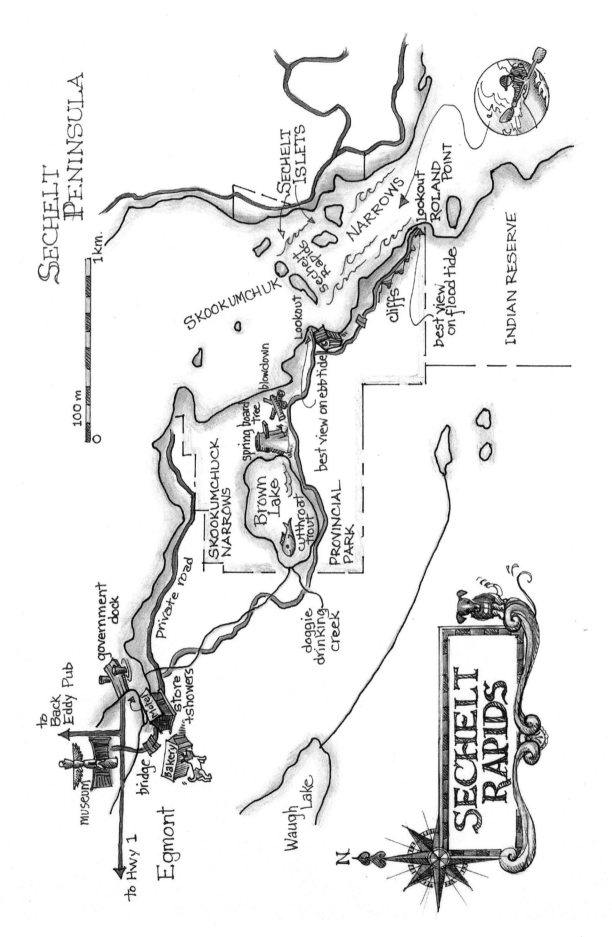

SECHELT PENINSULA

Sechelt Islets

SKOOKUMCHUK

Sechelt Rapids

NARROWS

Lookout

ROLAND POINT

best view on flood tide

INDIAN RESERVE

cliffs

blowdown

Lookout

SKOOKUMCHUCK NARROWS

spring board tree

best view on ebb tide

Brown Lake

cutthroat trout

PROVINCIAL PARK

Private road

government dock

doggie drinking creek

to Back Eddy Pub

Motel

store + showers

Bakery

museum

bridge

to Hwy 1

Egmont

Waugh Lake

1 km.

100 m

0

SECHELT RAPIDS

N

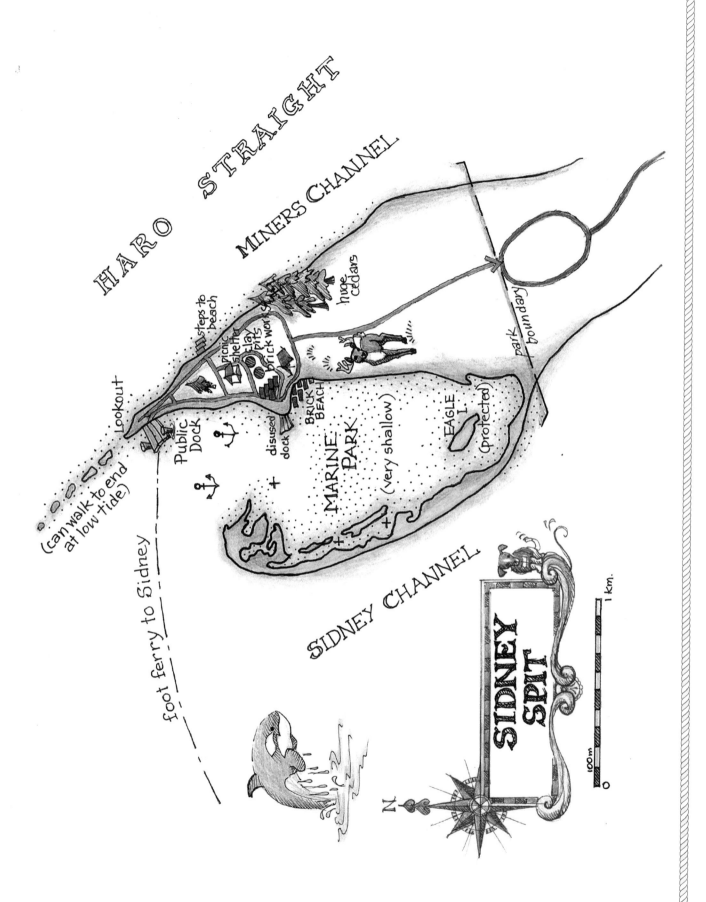

HARO STRAIGHT

MINERS CHANNEL

park boundary

steps to beach

huge cedars

picnic shelter

clay pits

brick works

Lookout

(can walk to end at low tide)

Public Dock

disused dock

BRICK BEACH

MARINE PARK

(very shallow)

EAGLE I. (protected)

foot ferry to Sidney

SIDNEY CHANNEL

SIDNEY SPIT

N

1 km.

100 m

0

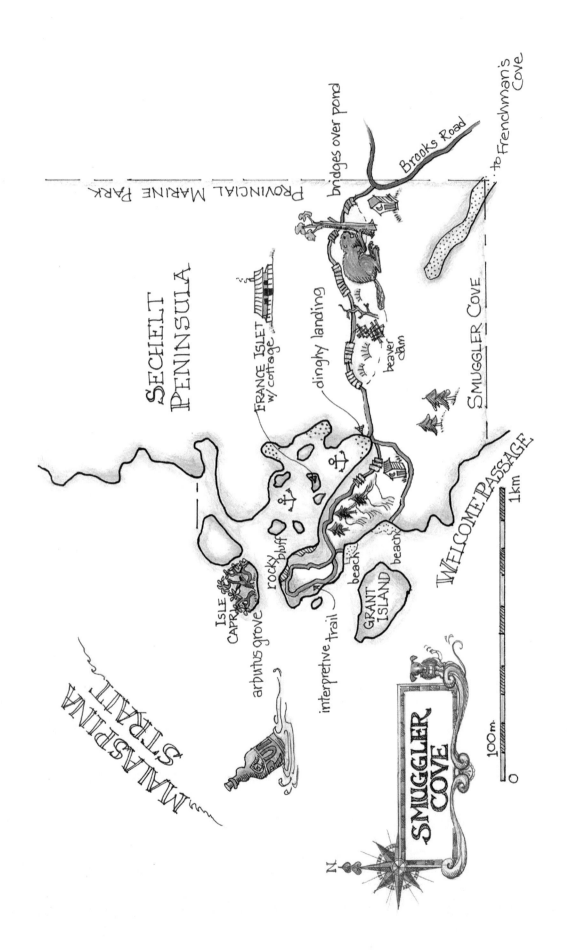

MALASPINA STRAIT

SECHELT PENINSULA

PROVINCIAL MARINE PARK

bridges over pond

Brooks Road

to Frenchman's Cove

SMUGGLER COVE

beaver dam

dinghy landing

FRANCE ISLET w/cottage

Isle CAPRI

arbutus grove

rocky bluff

interpretive trail

beach

GRANT ISLAND

beach

WELCOME PASSAGE

1km

SMUGGLER COVE

100 m.

0

N

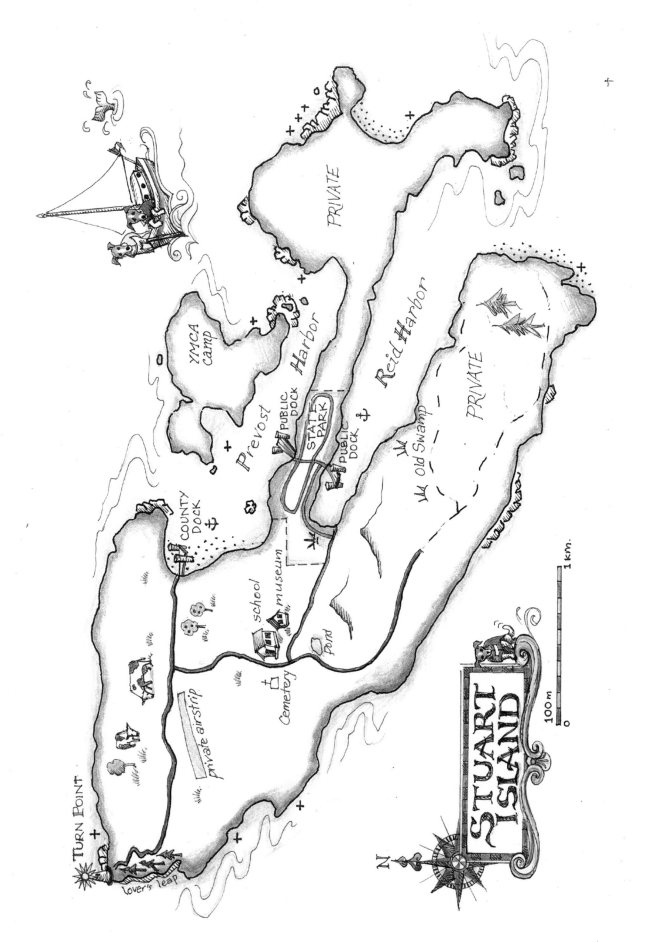

STUART ISLAND

PRIVATE

PRIVATE

PRIVATE

Reid Harbor

Prevost Harbor

YMCA Camp

PUBLIC DOCK

STATE PARK

PUBLIC DOCK

COUNTY DOCK

old Swamp

school

museum

pond

Cemetery

private airstrip

TURN POINT

lover's leap

N

100 m

0

1 km.

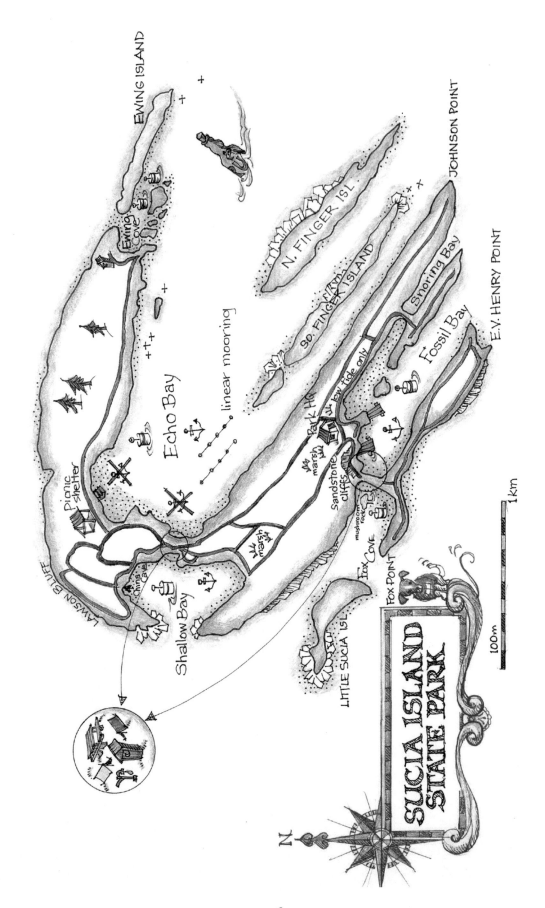

EWING ISLAND

EWING ISLAND

JOHNSON POINT

N. FINGER ISL.

Ewing Cove

So. FINGER ISLAND

linear mooring

Snoring Bay

E.V. HENRY POINT

Echo Bay

Fossil Bay

low tide only

Park Hq.

Picnic shelter

marsh

Sandstone cliffs

LAWSON BLUFF

China Cave

Mushroom rock

Shallow Bay

marsh

Fox Cove

Fox Point

LITTLE SUCIA ISL.

1 km

100m

SUCIA ISLAND
STATE PARK

N

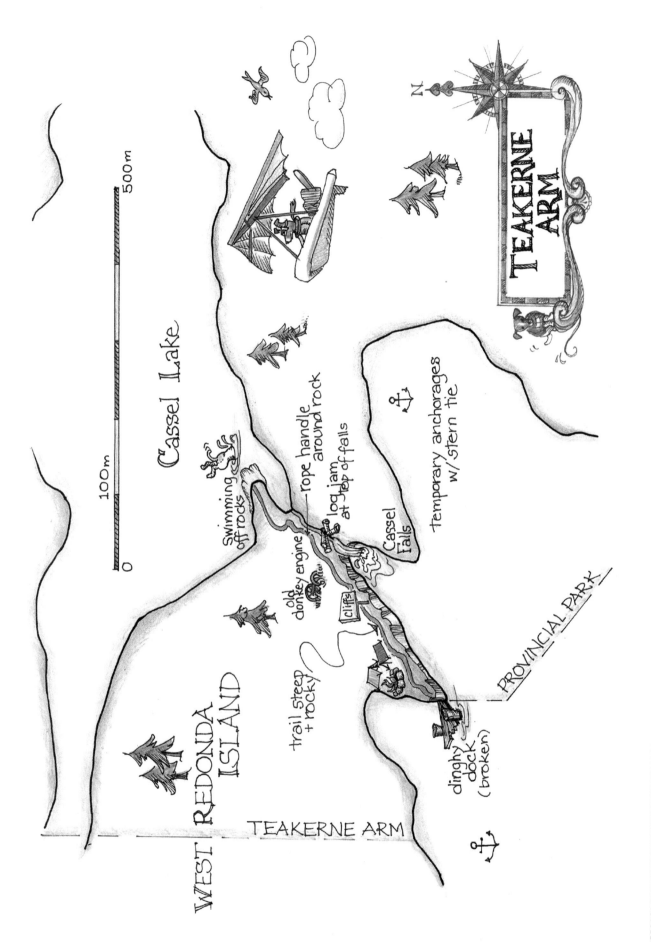

WEST REDONDA ISLAND

TEAKERNE ARM

Cassel Lake

TEAKERNE ARM

500m

100m

0

Swimming off rocks

old donkey engine

cliffs

rope handle around rock

log jam at top of falls

Cassel Falls

trail steep + rocky

dinghy dock (broken)

temporary anchorages w/stern tie

PROVINCIAL PARK

N

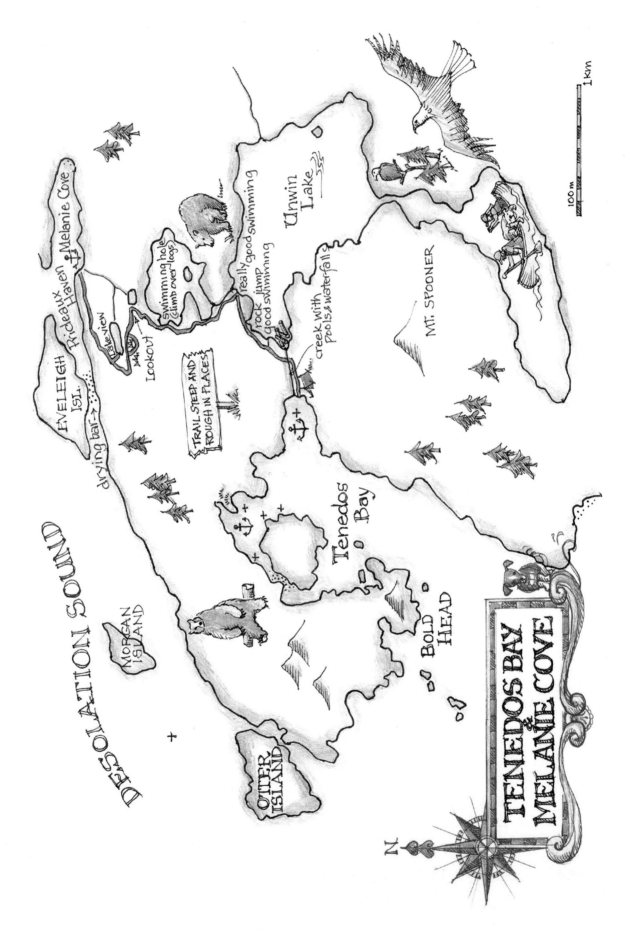

DESOLATION SOUND

EVELEIGH ISL.

Prideaux Haven ⚓ Melanie Cove

Lakeview

Lookout

drying bar →

Swimming hole (climb over logs)

really good swimming

rock jump good swimming

Unwin Lake

creek with pools & waterfalls

MT. SPOONER

TRAIL STEEP AND ROUGH IN PLACES

MORGAN ISLAND

Tenedos Bay

Bold Head

OTTER ISLAND

TENEDOS BAY & MELANIE COVE

N

100 m

1 km

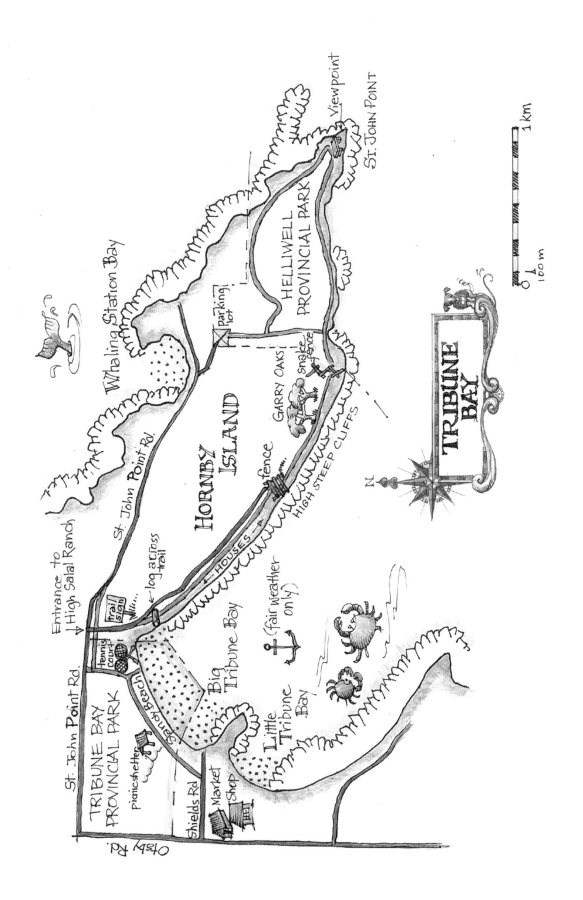

HORNBY ISLAND

TRIBUNE BAY

Viewpoint

St. John Point

HELLIWELL PROVINCIAL PARK

Whaling Station Bay

Parking lot

Snake fence

Garry Oaks

fence

HIGH STEEP CLIFFS

St. John Point Rd.

Entrance to High Salal Ranch

log across trail

Trail sign

HOUSES

(fair weather only)

Big Tribune Bay

Little Tribune Bay

Sandy Beach

Tennis court

TRIBUNE BAY PROVINCIAL PARK

St. John Point Rd.

Picnic shelter

Shields Rd

Market Shop

Ostby Rd.

N

100m 0

1 km

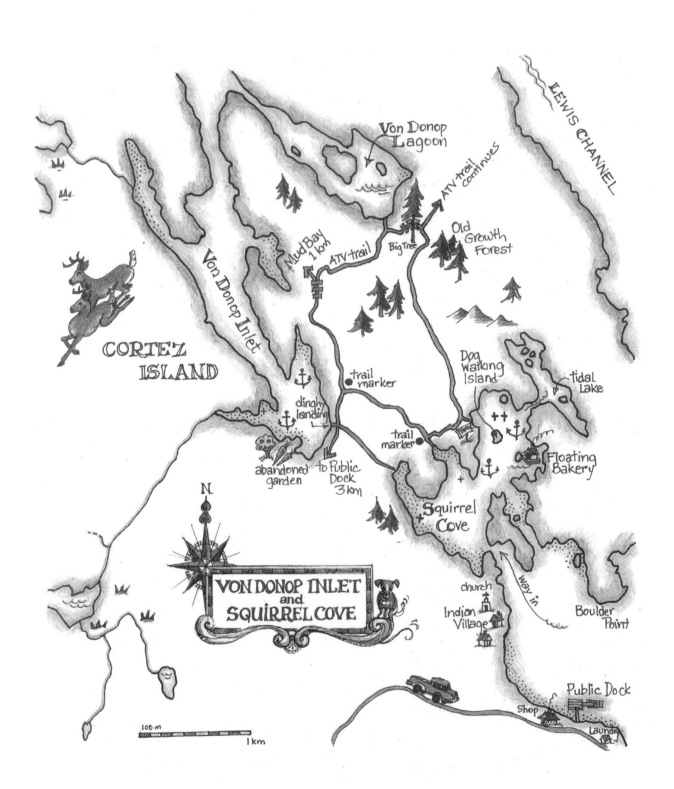

LEWIS CHANNEL

Von Donop
Lagoon

ATV trail continues

ATV trail

Big Tree

Old Growth Forest

Mud Bay
1 km

Von Donop Inlet

CORTEZ
ISLAND

trail marker

Dog Walking Island

tidal Lake

dinghy landing

trail marker

Floating Bakery

abandoned garden

to Public Dock
3 km

Squirrel Cove

N

VON DONOP INLET
and
SQUIRREL COVE

church

Indian Village

way in

Boulder Point

100 m

1 km

Shop

Public Dock

Laundry

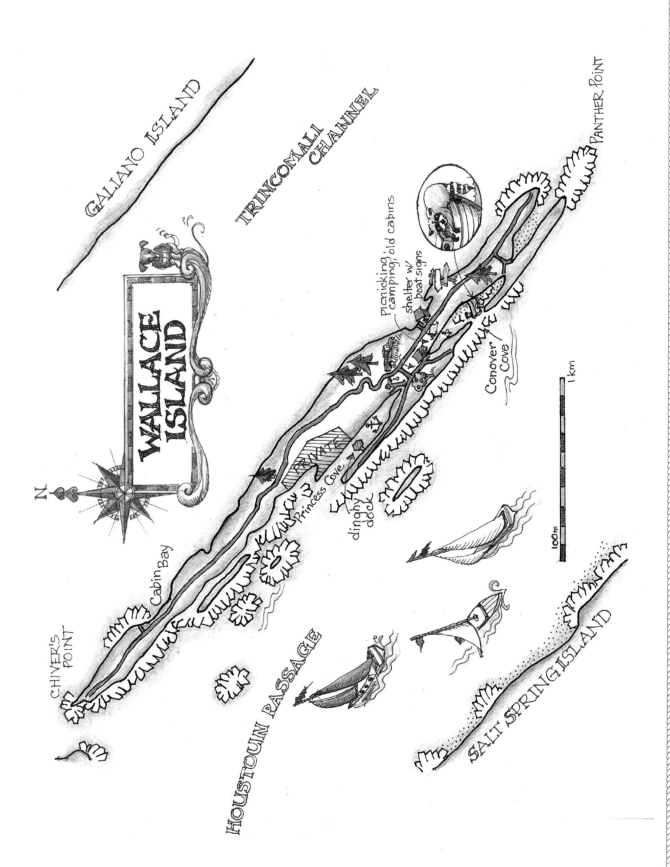

GALIANO ISLAND

TRINCOMALI CHANNEL

PANTHER POINT

WALLACE ISLAND

N

Picnicking, camping, old cabins

shelter w/ boat signs

Conover Cove

Cabin Bay

CHIVER'S POINT

Princess Cove

dinghy dock

PRIVATE

1 km

100m

HOUSTOUN PASSAGE

SALT SPRING ISLAND